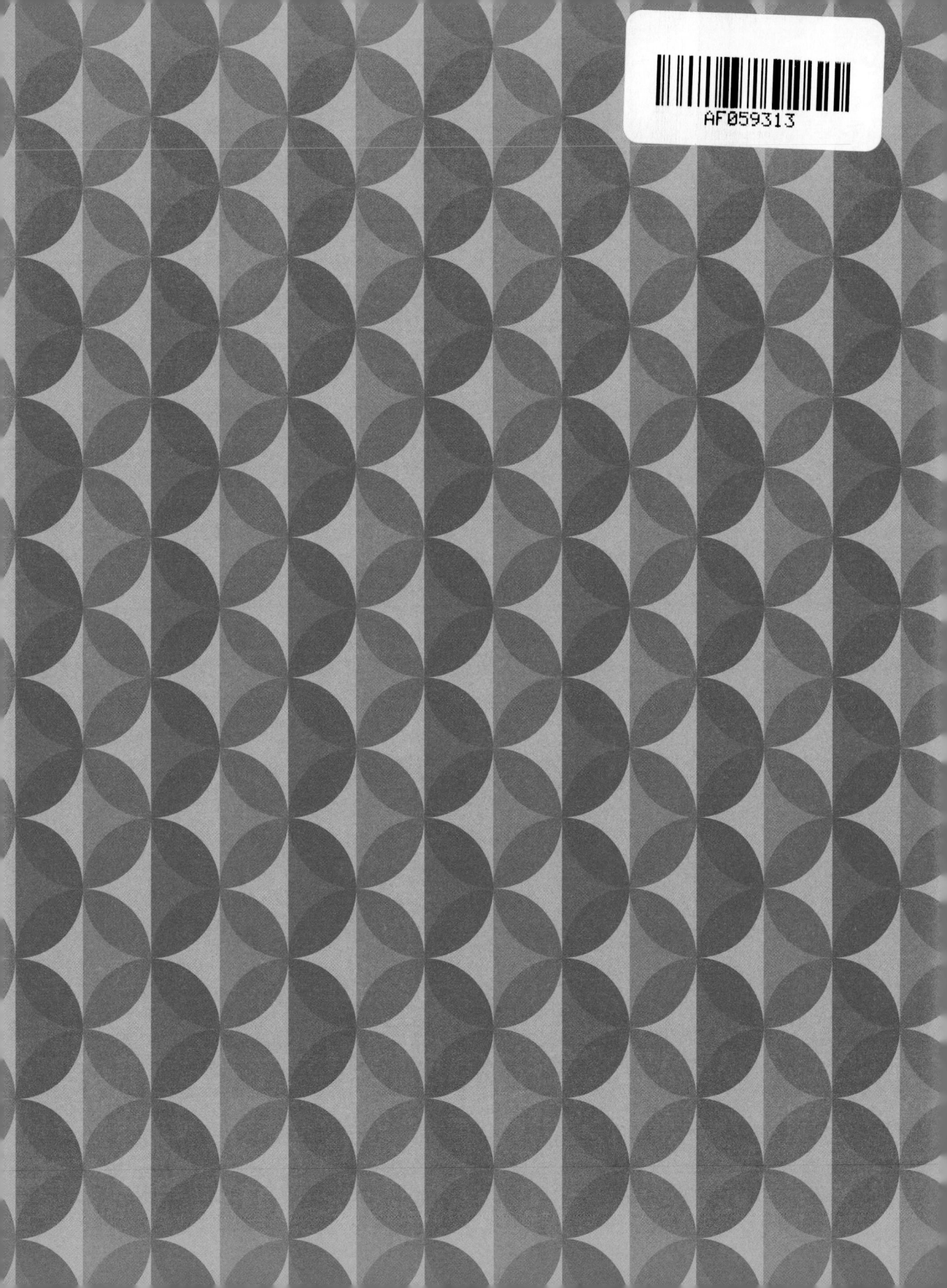

A YEAR OF colour

For Jules, who is my colour

Quarto

First published in 2026 by Frances Lincoln,
an imprint of The Quarto Group.
One Triptych Place, London, SE1 9SH,
United Kingdom
T (0)20 7700 9000
www.Quarto.com

EEA Representation, WTS Tax d.o.o., Žanova ulica 3, 4000 Kranj, Slovenia
www.wts-tax.si

Text Copyright © 2026 Ann-Marie Powell
Photographs Copyright © 2026 Julie Skelton; except for front cover photograph Copyright © 2026 Penny Walker
Design Copyright © 2026 Quarto Publishing plc

Ann-Marie Powell has asserted her moral right to be identified as the Author of this Work in accordance with the Copyright Designs and Patents Act 1988.

All rights reserved. No part of this book may be reproduced or utilised in any form or by any means, electronic or mechanical, including photocopying, recording or by any information storage and retrieval system, without permission in writing from Frances Lincoln.

Every effort has been made to trace the copyright holders of material quoted in this book. If application is made in writing to the publisher, any omissions will be included in future editions.

A catalogue record for this book is available from the British Library.

ISBN 978-1-83600-350-2
Ebook ISBN 978-1-83600-351-9

10 9 8 7 6 5 4 3 2 1

Design by Sarah Pyke

Publisher Philip Cooper
Editorial Director Alice Graham
Managing Editor Laura Bulbeck
Senior Designer Isabel Eeles
Senior Production Controller Rohana Yusof

Printed in Guangdong, China TT102025

Editorial Note
All the photography in this book was taken at the author's home in Hampshire, UK. Every effort has been made to provide broad planting advice, but you may need to adapt to the conditions of your garden.

Front cover *Verbascum* 'Petra'; *Lonicera* 'Purple Storm'; *Geum* 'Totally Tangerine'; *Sanguisorba officinalis* 'Lum'; *Craspedia globosa*; *Baptisia* 'Burgundy Blast'.

Contents *Verbascum chaixii* 'Sixteen Candles'; *Agastache* 'Blackadder'; *Crocosmia × crocosmiiflora* 'George Davison'; *Coreopsis tinctoria* 'Radiata Tigrina'; *Verbena bonariensis*.

A YEAR OF colour

How to create a bold and bright garden

Ann-Marie Powell
Photography by Julie Skelton

Contents

Real Garden Colour — 06

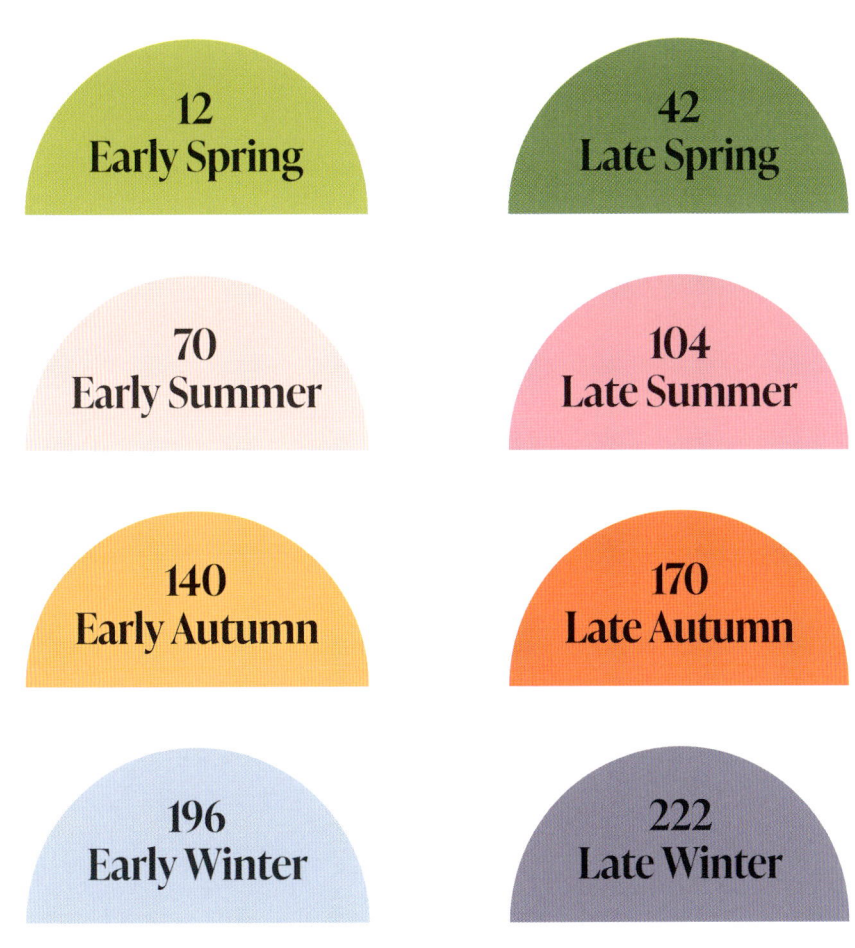

12 Early Spring
42 Late Spring
70 Early Summer
104 Late Summer
140 Early Autumn
170 Late Autumn
196 Early Winter
222 Late Winter

Plant Directory — 250
General Index — 253
About the Author & Photographer — 255
Acknowledgements — 256

Real Garden Colour

Some gardeners whisper about 'good taste' in hushed tones, and then there are those of us who believe that if your garden doesn't have you rushing to throw open the curtains each morning to see what new colourful blooming combination awaits, you're missing out on one of life's greatest pleasures.

If you've picked up this book, you're clearly in the 'gardens should be thrilling' camp – and I couldn't be more delighted. It took me far too long to stop worrying about what others might think of my bold colour choices and start embracing nature's glorious technicolour palette with the enthusiasm it deserves. Now I can't imagine gardening any other way.

Welcome to my garden – a glorious, unashamed celebration that's been carved out between the daily demands of work, family and everything else life insists on throwing our way. This isn't one of those immaculate gardens you see in magazines, photographed at dawn with professional lighting and not a slug trail in sight. This is a real garden, one that gets tended in snatched moments between meetings, weeded while supper simmers and planted with soil-caked fingers after days spent designing dream gardens for other people.

No matter how tired I am or how long my to-do list has grown, the sight of emerging shoots never fails to quicken my pulse. Each morning I step outside with my mug of tea, still in my dressing gown if I'm honest, to see what's newly opened overnight or which colourful blooms are catching the early light just right. These small daily rituals have become essential to me – moments of pure pleasure that set the tone for whatever challenges the day might hold.

The gardens I'm sharing require attention, care, and yes, a bit of effort. But here's the thing: that effort is part of the joy.

I find there's something deeply satisfying about deadheading dahlias on a summer evening, dividing perennials in autumn or the meditative quality of weeding a border. This hands-on approach has been crucial to me, especially in challenging times when gardening in full technicolour has helped me get through the year, month, week and sometimes even just the hour. When people ask me how I find the time, I explain that I don't find it – I make it, because the alternative of living without this daily burst of natural beauty has become unthinkable.

This book shares a year in a genuinely lived-in garden. It's about creating maximum impact with realistic effort, because let's be honest – none of us has unlimited hours to spend perfecting our plant combinations, no matter how much we might fantasise about such luxury. Through its pages, I share not just what I've learned through three decades of professional garden design, but the spectacular colour and most successful combinations from my own garden, where the only clients I need to satisfy are me, the bees and butterflies.

The garden I'm sharing with you isn't vast – it is roughly 10 x 20 metres (33 x 66 feet), with front and back a similar size but entirely different aspects and moods. The rear is east-facing and split on two levels: an upper deck of gnarly old oak where I write and pot up plants, then six broad steps down to a circular lawn surrounded by packed borders. The front may face west, but the tree-lined, sunken lane we live on negates much of the sun we might otherwise expect, creating its own microclimate and challenges.

The principles in these pages work regardless of scale – whether you have vast borders or a collection of pots. I believe every planting spot should pulse with personality and deliver moments that make us gardeners gasp with delight. Every corner in my garden earns its keep, from the clustered pots around the back door that greet me each morning, to the challenging dry shade under our wildlife hedge – all of it has become my testing ground for experimental colour combinations.

The colours here are bold, unapologetic and occasionally gloriously over the top – exactly the kind of combinations that make gardening such fun. You'll find bright pink dahlias revelling next to purple salvias, acid-yellow euphorbias illuminating spring corners, and enough orange to horrify certain garden designers. These aren't colours lifted from coordinated paint charts or design theory textbooks. They're combinations that make me grin on dreary Monday mornings, that glow magnificently in evening sunshine and that provide essential fuel for the bees, butterflies and birds that share this space.

Through these pages, I want to share something deeper than just the infectious joy of gardening with colour – I hope you'll experience the same sense of elation, calm, hope and meditative peace that colour in my garden gives me every single day, regardless of the season. There's something profoundly grounding about this daily connection with nature's palette, and I'm determined to pass on that feeling through achievable plant combinations, a genuine sense of the seasons and the deep contentment that comes from tending something beautiful.

You'll discover over 40 tried and tested plant combinations, each with detailed growing advice and tips, plus practical guidance for every season – from sowing sweet peas in early winter to creating stunning dahlia displays in late summer. I've captured this garden at different moments throughout the year because colour isn't static – it's a constantly evolving performance where the cast changes with the seasons, the lighting shifts throughout the year, and moods move with the weather.

Most importantly, this book is about finding joy in everyday gardening. Not grand gestures requiring professional teams and bottomless budgets, but the simple pleasure of choosing plants that lift your spirits, combining colours that reflect your personality and creating a garden where nature's floral firework display welcomes you home each day.

So, settle down with a proper cup of tea (or something stronger if today's been particularly challenging) and join me for a year of colour that will transform how you see your garden's potential. I promise you'll discover not just tried and tested combinations, but the confidence to trust your instincts, experiment with your own variations and plant exactly what makes you happy. Because the most beautiful gardens aren't those that play it safe – they're the ones that pulse with authentic colour and the unmistakable stamp of someone who dared to be bold.

I promise you'll discover not just tried and tested combinations, but the confidence to trust your instincts, experiment with your own variations, and plant exactly what makes you happy

Early Spring

As spring begins, there's a special moment when the air suddenly feels different – fresher, fuller and somehow more alive. The light changes too; no longer the flat grey of winter but with a clarity that makes colours appear sharper, more defined. It's as if the world has been waiting for change, holding its breath and, at last, finally decides to exhale. The garden awakens tentatively, pushing exploratory shoots through cold soil to test the temperature before fully committing to growth. This is early spring – a season of cautious optimism, occasional setbacks and welcome surprises.

I find myself pulling on my boots and striding outside with increasing frequency now, peering at the ground to witness the first brave snowdrops and crocuses pushing through frost, rain and occasionally snow. These diminutive pioneers arrive with perfect timing, delivering concentrated bursts of attention-grabbing colour just when we need them most. Once up and out, these frontrunners are swiftly followed by the cheerful trumpets of early narcissi and the jewel-like tones of *Iris reticulata*, creating puddles of colour that seem to swell and intensify day by day. The garden unfolds like a letter from an old friend, revealing its news bit by bit – each paragraph offering fresh surprises as tales are shared at their own pace, making you excited to read what comes next.

This awakening brings a quiet reassurance that nature keeps its promises, even after the longest winter. I notice my step becoming lighter as I wander through the garden with my morning cuppa, spotting new shoots and unfurling leaves, mentally cataloguing what's emerging and what's still dormant. Scatterings of primrose, snowdrops hovering through the front

Early spring's bridging plants shoulder winter aside – *Iris reticulata* 'Angela' in palest blue, deeper 'Pauline' and winter aconites bringing life to pots when we need it most

garden borders and the beaks of other bulbs peaking from the soil everywhere I look. It's a daily treasure hunt, with rewards that increase exponentially as the weeks pass.

Though spring's plant selection is narrower than summer's extensive range, the result is that each performer chosen carries greater impact. For reliable flower-power in these tentative weeks, certain plants deserve prime positions. Rather than in the ground, I scatter the rich purple cups of *Crocus tommasinianus* generously through my pots, where I can enjoy them up close, their heads raised and in sight of my kitchen windows like a gentle purple haze, as their cousin, the bold and vibrant *Crocus olivieri* subsp. *balansae* 'Orange Monarch', promenades around the lawn. Both are my rear garden joys, while in the front, the beautiful nodding bells of an increasing array of snowdrop varieties (*Galanthus nivalis*) shine beneath the trees, accompanied by beaming faces of winter aconites (*Eranthis hyemalis*), their acid-yellow flowers set off perfectly by a frill of green bracts. I can't help but smile back at them.

I prefer to keep spring close by my side, better enjoyed by its proximity, so I incorporate early-flowering varieties of *Helleborus orientalis* in the borders near the house. Their quietly nodding flowers in shades of slate, plum and soft pink add sophisticated notes of colour among emerging perennials. Their leathery evergreen foliage provides valuable structure during winter's lean months before being cut away to reveal their colourful blooms. Plant them where they'll be backlit by morning or evening light to fully appreciate the glow of their translucent petals.

The emerging foliage of herbaceous perennials adds another dimension to the early spring palette. The bronze fronds of *Dryopteris erythrosora* unfurl like coppery question marks, while

This awakening brings a quiet reassurance that nature keeps its promises, even after the longest winter

Hellebores have watched and waited, their speckled heads as in thrall as we are, finally turning to greet the strengthening sun – this is the moment early spring truly begins

the crimson shoots of peonies push through the soil like sharpened pencils.

For years, I turned up my nose at daffodils, thinking them gaudy, too brash, too yellow. But thankfully I was won over by the extraordinary diversity of narcissi in all their forms. From pure whites to subtle creams, peachy pinks to salmon oranges, modern daffodils offer a palette that extends well beyond yellow. There are miniatures perfect for pot toppers, elegantly simple varieties for naturalistic settings, and flamboyant doubles that resemble peonies, all of which bring joy in spades as they boldly trumpet in the arrival of spring. And then, of course, there's their extraordinary scent.

In larger country gardens, I love establishing more extensive displays of daffodils that take advantage of the generous space. Sweeping drifts of *Narcissus* 'W.P. Milner', 'Actaea' and the wild British native *Narcissus* 'Lobularis' naturalised in grass to weave rivers of gold at the edges of lawns, through meadows and beneath still-bare deciduous trees.

In more compact urban gardens, containers become essential for early spring colour impact. Strategically placed near entrances and seating areas, these miniature seasonal showcases can be layered with early-flowering *Narcissus* 'Tête-à-tête' and the hoop petticoat

N. bulbocodium 'Arctic Bells', topped with violas and wallflowers. I also find a large pot near the front door holding a structural evergreen such as sweet box (*Sarcococca confusa*) offers both fragrance and visual delight – a welcoming committee for visitors and a daily pleasure for those that live there.

The early spring garden rewards our patience through winter with the spill of a new season, best enjoyed close up. For me, this time of year is not about grand, sweeping displays but rather intimate moments of discovery – finding the first bumblebee visiting hellebore flowers, noticing how morning dew catches on emerging foliage, appreciating the subtle colour variations in petals, building anticipation for the more exuberant seasons to come. Planting for spring means you shake off winter's grasp earlier than you otherwise might, to witness it reawakening for another year of growth, colour and endless possibility. What could be better than celebrating each small miracle as nature's cycle begins anew?

Opposite and Above You can almost feel the garden gathering itself for the show ahead – daffodils pushing through pots, fresh growth emerging in every corner, the *Amelanchier* (and neighbourhood cat!) presiding over it all

Golden Woodland Tapestry

Early bulbs and perennials for dappled shade

In the quiet corners where garden meets woodland and light meets shade, this buttery combination forms a luminous understorey that brightens gloomy corners from early to mid-spring. The nodding flowers of *Erythronium* 'Pagoda' dance above airy sprays of *Epimedium* × *versicolor* 'Sulphureum', while *Narcissus* 'Bella Estrella' adds height and fragrance. Soon, *Tulipa* 'Green Mile' will join the performance with its distinctive yellow-green goblets licked with green flames.

What makes this combination sing is the interplay of yellow tones against varied foliage textures beneath deciduous trees, where spring sunlight filters through bare branches. Each plant emerges in sequence, creating a display that evolves from early to late spring – just when we're most desperate for garden joy. The mottled leaves of dog's tooth violet (*Erythronium dens-canis*) and bronze-tinted, heart-shaped foliage of the *Epimedium* provide additional visual interest, making this combination work twice as hard in those tricky dry, shady spots that most gardeners find difficult.

> **TIPS FOR SUCCESS**
> - Prepare the ground with plenty of leaf mould to mimic natural woodland conditions – these plants thrive in humus-rich but well-drained soil.
> - Drop individual groups of bulbs from waist height and plant exactly where they fall for a naturally random effect that looks as though Mother Nature herself arranged them.
> - For the *Epimedium*, commit to a late winter haircut. It makes all the difference between a scruffy mess and a breath-taking display of fresh foliage and flowers.
> - Allow bulb foliage to die back naturally – those yellowing leaves may look tatty but they're busy feeding next year's bulbs and flower display.

Erythronium 'Pagoda' This aristocrat of spring bulbs produces multiple lily-like golden-yellow blooms per stem, each with elegantly recurved petals that hover above glossy, mottled foliage. A robust hybrid with excellent garden staying power, it gradually naturalises in humus-rich soil and dappled shade. Plant the bulbs 10cm (4in) deep in autumn and resist disturbing them – they're rather particular about being moved once established. HARDINESS: RHS H5

***Epimedium* × *versicolor* 'Sulphureum'**
The ultimate problem-solver for dry shade, this ground-covering perennial brings two seasonal treats – delicate sprays of pale yellow 'fairy wings' on wiry stems and heart-shaped leaves that emerge with stunning bronze-red tints before maturing to mid-green. Once established, it laughs in the face of drought and root competition from nearby trees. HARDINESS: RHS H7

***Narcissus* 'Bella Estrella'** This charming daffodil (whose Spanish name aptly translates as 'beautiful star') bears pristine white segments surrounding split cups of soft yellow with delicately frilled edges. What makes it exceptional is its lovely fragrance and habit of producing multiple flowers per stem. The strong, upright stems create the perfect airy middle layer in this woodland composition. In, truth, it's perhaps my favourite daffodil. HARDINESS: RHS H6

***Tulipa* 'Green Mile'** Adding zing to this woodland scene, this RHS Award of Garden Merit winner from the Viridiflora Group presents sophisticated yellow blooms with prominent lime-green striping and slightly feathered edges. Its architectural, upright form provides valuable vertical accents as spring progresses. Unlike many tulips, 'Green Mile' performs well in partial shade and can return reliably if planted in well-drained soil. HARDINESS: RHS H6

Unfurling Drama

Textures for shady borders

Before the first proper flowers appear, it's all about the textures – the tightly coiled fiddleheads of *Matteuccia* poking through last year's mulch, unfurling like prehistoric creatures, together with the *Rodgersia*'s bronze, chestnut-like leaves emerging from the soil with such intention and confidence.

What works well is the contrast between forms, from the delicate fern croziers to the bold, pleated surface of *Rodgersia*, while the colour palette of copper, mahogany and fresh green provides visual interest just as the garden begins to awake.

My shrub rose might be nameless (inherited with the garden and never properly identified), but that doesn't stop it putting on a splendid show of burgundy-flushed new growth.

Matteuccia struthiopteris I'll never grow tired of these ferns as they emerge – first, as tight little coils, then gradually unfurling into those elegant vases. Despite looking so delicate, they're surprisingly tough customers; mine have soldiered on through some pretty neglectful summers. Just give them room – they do spread! **HARDINESS: RHS H5**

Shrub Rose (emerging foliage) Gardening books never mention how gorgeous rose leaves are in spring. Before there's even a whisper of a bud, those polished, red-tinted leaflets unfold with a glossiness that's quite special. This one produces particularly vivid new growth that holds its colour for a good few weeks before settling into summer green. Worth growing even if it never flowered, though thankfully it does, in orange. **HARDINESS: RHS H6**

Rodgersia podophylla **'Braunlaub'** My absolute favourite for borders with less direct sunlight. Its massive, palm-like leaves emerge chocolate-bronze before gradually greening up as summer progresses. I've let it run through the border in clumps, editing out any bits that pop up in inconvenient spots. Not a plant for tiny gardens (see Tips for success for an alternative variety), but perfect for adding some architecture to a shady spot. **HARDINESS: RHS H6**

TIPS FOR SUCCESS

- Embrace moisture – none of these plants will thank you for drought conditions. A good spring mulch helps keep things consistently damp without becoming waterlogged.
- Allow space for maturity – especially for the *Matteuccia* and *Rodgersia*. They'll both reach impressive proportions given time, so resist the temptation to crowd them initially.
- If space is at a premium, substitute *Rodgersia pinnata* 'Chocolate Wing' – a more manageable variety that maintains a smaller footprint, and *Dryopteris erythrosora* instead of the *Matteuccia*, which offers similar feathery texture at a more modest 45–60cm (1½–2ft) height.

Gold & Sapphire

Bulbs for an early spring glow

Nothing lifts the spirits quite like pots bursting with spring bulbs. This combination brings together buttery yellows and electric blues – colours that celebrate each other in early spring sunshine. Four complementary narcissi varieties – 'Avalon', 'Moonlight Sensation', 'Flower Drift' and miniature 'Tête-à-Tête' – create a foundation, accented by blue anemones. I layer a few of these daffodils and the other bulbs in one large pot to bloom at different times – see Tips for Success on p.26 – and create a succession of flowers. The weathered terracotta containers add warmth, while amelanchier blossom provides an airy frame.

This display works in semi-shade or full sun and in any garden, regardless of soil type, making it perfect for space-saving containers on decks, balconies or patios. The sequence begins with 'Tête-à-Tête', followed by the larger daffodils, with anemones and grape hyacinths (*Muscari*) completing the picture as we move into mid-spring.

Narcissus **'Avalon'** This large-cupped daffodil produces outward-facing blooms with pristine yellow petals and frilled cream cups. Each bulb typically produces multiple blooms, creating generous clusters that stand up well to spring showers. Plant 15cm (6in) deep for the best flowering performance. **HARDINESS: RHS H6**

Narcissus **'Moonlight Sensation'** The pale lemon-yellow flowers of this variety glow in evening light, creating a luminous presence in spring containers. Its slightly reflexed petals and neat cup give a more sophisticated silhouette than traditional daffodils. Wonderfully scented, it's perfect for placing near seating areas. **HARDINESS: RHS H6**

Narcissus **'Flower Drift'** This charming multi-headed variety produces clusters of semi-double blooms with creamy-white petals surrounding frilled yellow-orange centres. Each stem carries several flowers, creating abundant displays in containers. The blooms also have a rich, spicy fragrance and add textural contrast to the single narcissi in the collection. **HARDINESS: RHS H6**

Narcissus **'Tête-à-Tête'** The ever-reliable miniature that starts the spring show. Each bulb produces multiple stems carrying cheerful golden-yellow flowers with slightly darker cups. At just 15–20cm (6–8in) tall, it's perfect for the container edge or smaller pots. Always the first to flower, it's robustly weather resistant. **HARDINESS: RHS H6**

Anemone coronaria **(De Caen Group) 'Mister Fokker'** Intense cobalt-blue saucers with black-button centres create dramatic punctuation among the softer yellows. These anemones perform brilliantly in the sharp drainage that pots provide, opening only on sunny days. It always amazes me that such gnarly looking corms produce such beautiful blooms. **HARDINESS: RHS H5**

→

Muscari latifolium In my opinion, this two-tone grape hyacinth is one of the best, each flower spike dark navy at the bottom, transitioning to a lighter sky blue at the top. It provides that essential lower layer to the container display and complements the colour of the anemones. **HARDINESS: RHS H6**

Amelanchier × lamarckii Acting as a backdrop to the composition, this small tree's star-shaped white blossoms arrive at precisely the right moment to complement the container display. Later, coppery young leaves and summer berries will extend interest long after the spring bulbs have faded. **HARDINESS: RHS H7**

> ### TIPS FOR SUCCESS
> - In autumn, layer bulbs in a large pot according to size, with the larger daffodils deepest, anemones in the middle, and muscari near the top for a perfectly sequenced spring display. 'Tête-à-Tête' can go near the top, too, or plant in separate small pots.
> - Allow foliage to die back naturally after flowering, as the yellowing leaves are feeding next year's display.
> - Terracotta pots dry out quickly, so keep an eye on watering during the spring growing period, particularly in warmer spells.
> - Bulbs may not flower as well in subsequent years if kept in a pot. If yours are not performing as they should, after flowering, when the leaves have faded, replant the bulbs in a border. Prior to moving them, feed with liquid fertiliser to ensure a good display the following year.

Narcissus 'Flower Drift'

Anemone coronaria (De Caen Group) 'Mister Fokker'

Narcissus 'Avalon'

Amelanchier × *lamarckii*

Muscari latifolium with *Narcissus* 'Tête-à-Tête'

Flame & Fire

Border tulips with staying power

When tulips hit their stride in mid-spring, nothing quite matches their bold presence and saturated colours. This fiery combination brings together flame-streaked lily-flowered 'Ballerina', bicoloured 'Banja Luka', rich orange-red 'Bourbon Street', deep maroon-purple 'Continental' and elegant 'Sonnet', their warm tones creating a sophisticated palette that glows in the mid-spring sunshine.

The real triumph here is their reliable return for a third consecutive year in the border – proving that with the right varieties and conditions, tulips needn't be treated as annuals. Planted in well-drained soil in full sun, these varieties have thrived without lifting, the mix of flower shapes – from classic goblets to pointed lily forms – adding textural interest to the borders before the perennials appear.

If you'd like to grow tulips as perennials, consider Fosteriana, Kaufmanniana and Greigii groups, all renowned for returning year after year? Species tulips and their close hybrids also naturalise effectively, gradually forming colonies that improve with each passing year, given the right conditions.

Tulipa **'Banja Luka'** This dramatic Darwin hybrid tulip produces large goblet-shaped blooms with a striking bicolour pattern – golden-yellow petals feathered and flamed with red. Its robust nature makes it one of the more reliable tulips for a border, returning consistently in my garden every year. HARDINESS: RHS H6

Tulipa **'Ballerina'** An elegant lily-flowered variety with pointed, reflexed petals in glowing orange with subtle yellow edging. The slender flowers sway gracefully in spring breezes and emit a delightful sweet fragrance, unusual among tulips. Its reliable perennial performance makes it a border mainstay. HARDINESS: RHS H6

Tulipa **'Sonnet'** This sophisticated tulip presents elongated blooms in a soft pinky-purple flushed with apricot and yellow flames, creating a watercolour effect. The elegant flowers stand on strong stems above the straight, blue-green foliage. Performs reliably as a returning border tulip in well-drained conditions. HARDINESS: RHS H6

Tulipa **'Continental'** A classic-shaped tulip with rounded, maroon-purple blooms that hold their colour consistently throughout the flowering period. Its medium height makes it perfect for the middle layer of a border planting, while its perennial nature ensures it builds impact year on year. HARDINESS: RHS H6

Tulipa **'Bourbon Street'** This dramatic variety provides the orange-red shades at the edge of the planting scheme here, adding depth and interest. The classic cup-shaped flowers with their rich, saturated colour create perfect contrast against the yellows. Another dependable tulip returner. HARDINESS: RHS H6

> **TIPS FOR SUCCESS**
> - Plant tulips deeply – 20cm (8in) rather than the standard 15cm (6in) helps perennialisation and protects from frost damage.
> - Ensure excellent drainage by selecting the right position or adding grit to heavy soils for long-term success.
> - Feed with balanced fertiliser in early spring and again after flowering to build bulb strength for next year.
> - Allow foliage to die back completely before removing – the yellowing leaves are replenishing the bulbs for future displays.

Pale & Interesting

Early spring's understated beauty

Just when winter feels like it will never end, these diminutive harbingers appear, creating subtle scatterings of colour on the woodland floor, which after a few years become rivers. The bright azure stars of *Scilla sardensis* intertwine with the soft primrose blooms of *Primula vulgaris,* joining the nodding white bells of *Scilla siberica* 'Alba', each playing their part in waking up the woodland amid a miniature forest of emerging daffodil spears.

This planting thrives in the dappled conditions of my front garden, where winter sun reaches the ground before tree canopies come into leaf. The bulbs return reliably each year and are gradually forming generous drifts with minimum input from me, while the primroses spread themselves about through self-seeding. What makes this combination special is its quiet confidence – these aren't showy divas, but their delicate arrival whispers to we winter-weary gardeners promises of the gardening year to come.

Scilla sardensis These azure-blue stars bring unexpected life to early spring gardens. Each slender stem carries several small outward-facing flowers with tiny white centres, creating pools of colour at ground level. Happy in light shade, they gradually form substantial colonies through both bulb division and self-seeding. Plant 5cm (2in) deep in autumn in deep, rich soil. **HARDINESS: RHS H6**

Primula vulgaris This primrose offers gentle cream-yellow flowers that seem to glow in the early spring garden. They often arrive uninvited, as blow-ins, the crinkled, spoon-shaped leaves forming a neat rosette from which the stemless flowers emerge on individual short stalks. Preferring cool, moist conditions, they're perfect woodland-edge plants that thrive in partial shade, and are always welcome here. **HARDINESS: RHS H7**

Scilla siberica **'Alba'** The pure white form of the Siberian squill creates pinpoints of sharp light, ensuring they provide impact despite their diminutive size. Each stem carries 1–3 nodding bell-shaped flowers above strap-like foliage. Though less assertive than its vibrant blue cousin, the white form illuminates shady spots and combines beautifully with both blues and yellows. **HARDINESS: RHS H6**

> **TIPS FOR SUCCESS**
> - Plant these early bulbs in autumn at three times their depth, adding a handful of grit beneath each bulb in heavier soils.
> - Allow bulb foliage to die back naturally after flowering to build strength for next year's display.
> - Primroses benefit from division every 3 years to maintain vigour – the best time is right after flowering.
> - Consider adding hellebores to extend the season and provide larger architectural elements alongside these diminutive plants.

Primula vulgaris **(top left)**; *Scilla siberica* 'Alba' **(top right)**; *Scilla sardensis* in the foreground, with a backdrop of *Primula vulgaris* **(bottom)**

Spring Jewels

Tulips to warm shady spots

The tulips here create a breathtaking spectacle in late spring against the backdrop of still-dormant rhododendrons, the perfect warm-up to the shrubs' later flowering. This boldly theatrical grouping includes the flame-licked 'Devenish', with its striking red-and-yellow flaring; the rich double 'Oakheart' in ochre-orange tones; dramatic purple 'Purple Heart'; and the delicately fringed 'Louvre Orange', with the elegant 'Cairo' adding its own dusty umber tones to enrich the scene further.

Surprisingly, this combination thrives in my woodland-edge setting where dappled shade provides relief from the hottest part of the day, while the evening and morning light allows for strong stems and vibrant colours. That's not to say some of the stems don't flop, but that adds to the theatre in my opinion. Additional varieties waiting in the wings include 'Avignon', graceful lily-flowered 'Ballerina', velvet-dark 'Queen of Night', 'Ridgedale', 'Slawa' and 'Uncle Tom' – creating a succession of blooms that extends the display of jewel-like tones against the backdrop of evergreen foliage.

Tulipa **'Devenish'** This showstopper features large crimson-red blooms dramatically edged with golden-yellow, creating a flame-like effect that glows. The goblet-shaped flowers stand proud on strong stems, making them perfect for both garden impact and cutting. Performs beautifully against the rhododendron backdrop. **HARDINESS: RHS H6**

Tulipa **'Oakheart'** A magnificent double tulip with richly layered petals in a smouldering blend of amber, orange and bronze. Each flower resembles a small peony, creating substantial visual weight to the planting scheme. The sturdy stems support the heavy blooms well, making it tough enough to stand up to heavy spring showers. **HARDINESS: RHS H6**

Tulipa **'Purple Heart'** This regal variety provides crucial colour contrast, with its deep aubergine-purple goblets held on tall, sturdy stems. The dark blooms create dramatic punctuation among the fiery tones of its companions, while echoing the shadows beneath the rhododendrons. The petals have a subtle sheen that catches the light beautifully. **HARDINESS: RHS H6**

Tulipa **'Louvre Orange'** The crystalline fringing on this tulip's petal edges creates a wonderful textural froth. The rich orange blooms, deepening to terracotta at their base, appear backlit when the sun shines through them. A beautiful bridge between the simpler forms elsewhere in the planting. **HARDINESS: RHS H6**

Tulipa **'Cairo'** Sleek and elegant blooms in warm, coppery orange with subtle yellow flaming, this tulip's classic goblet shape and medium height makes it an excellent supporting player that ties together the more dramatic varieties. The rich colour intensifies as the flower matures, adding depth to the overall display. **HARDINESS: RHS H6**

> **TIPS FOR SUCCESS**
> - When planting tulips near rhododendrons or other evergreen shrubs, ensure they receive sufficient light in spring. Turning your pots regularly will help.
> - Protect bulbs and emerging shoots from hungry wildlife, especially in woodland settings where squirrels and mice might like a nibble! In autumn, after planting, try covering susceptible bulbs with chicken wire pegged down with stones, removing it once the shoots have grown through the wire in spring, when they will be less appetising.
> - Follow the tips for other tulips (see p.28)

WHAT TO DO
EARLY SPRING

Early spring marks the transition from garden contemplation to garden action. This transitional period in our gardening year finally allows us to move from planning colour schemes and dreaming of plant combinations to preparing our gardens for the spectacular displays we've designed in our mind's eye. It's when we shake off winter's lethargy, sharpen our tools and set our gardens up for months of spectacular colour ahead – always maintaining that delicate balance of embracing new beginnings while protecting tender growth from late frosts. Each task completed now ensures your summer displays won't merely exist but hum with biodiversity and positively sing with vibrancy.

The Big Border Cut Back

Once temperatures consistently reach 10°C (50°F) or above, it's time for the big cut back – though not everything needs the chop. Cut back the ornamental grasses and herbaceous perennials that provided winter structure, but work in sections over several days rather than clearing everything at once. This staged approach allows overwintering beneficial insects time to relocate. Leave some seed heads for birds and wildlife until temperatures warm further. Rhythmic pruning makes way for fresh growth and creates neat piles of material for composting or chopping and dropping as mulch.

Early Protected Sowings

While it may still be too early for direct sowing, heated propagators become nurseries for the season ahead. Start tender perennials such as salvias, tithonia and rudbeckia, dahlias (from tubers), and half-hardy annuals requiring 14–16 weeks to reach planting size. That distinctive smell of tomato leaves from early seedlings – summer's promise in one whiff – makes even the most mundane windowsill feel like a professional nursery. Focus on plants that need longer growing periods now, before suitable outdoor planting conditions arrive.

Greenhouse Spring Clean

If you have a greenhouse, before filling it with trays of seedlings, give it the thorough clean it deserves. Remove plants stored overwinter temporarily to clean benches, wash glass inside and out to maximise spring light, and check for repairs needed. This preparation creates the perfect environment for nurturing all those seedlings that'll soon fill every available surface.

Soil Improvement and Bed Preparation

Early spring's freeze-thaw cycles make soil workable again, perfect for incorporating organic matter without causing compaction. Layer well-rotted compost or manure on the surface to improve the soil's structure, letting worm action carry it down to the depths, or gently forking it into the top 10cm (4in). Empty compost bins of finished material and use it

to mulch around permanent plantings, keeping it clear of stem bases, then begin filling them again with spring clean-up debris.

Early Plant Support Systems

As perennials emerge, install support structures while plants are still small. Bamboo canes, metal hoops or home-made brush supports work best when inserted early, allowing plants to grow through them naturally. Keep twine cut to manageable lengths in your pocket for quick securing jobs, avoiding the need to dash away and find the main ball!

Tool Preparation and Garden Audit

Before the gardening season intensifies, clean and sharpen all tools. Service mechanical equipment while demand for its use is low, and conduct a thorough garden assessment, noting winter damage, gaps in planting schemes and plants that need dividing later in the season.

First Lawn Maintenance

When grass begins active growth, give lawns their first gentle trim of the year. Keep blades at maximum height, carefully avoiding crocus foliage and other spring flowers that need time for their leaves to replenish their bulbs. This may be your final cut if participating in no mowing schemes later in the season. Rake out winter debris, aerate compacted areas if needed, and overseed thin patches while soil temperatures favour germination.

Plant Care Essentials

Check overwintered plants, refreshing the top layers of compost if they're in pots and removing

> **MY ESSENTIAL DOS AND DON'TS**
>
> + Start your dahlias off in a protected, frost-free spot.
> + Plant summer-flowering bulbs in well-prepared soil.
> + Install water butts to store rain for use later in the year.
> + Order biological pest controls before populations explode.
> + Sort or start off a composting area to create a circular system for seasonal clean-up materials.
> + Install plant supports proactively before growth accelerates.
> + Assess overwintered plants such as pelargoniums, providing fresh compost where needed.
> + Complete major garden planning while you can see where the holes in your borders are.
> + Keep feeding the birds.
> + Install nest boxes positioned away from high-activity areas.
> + Start protected seed sowing in pots or trays of quality, peat-free seed compost.
> + Apply slow-release fertiliser to trees, shrubs and hedges.
>
> − Cut back spring-flowering shrubs that bloom on the previous year's wood.
> − Plant frost-tender bedding before temperatures rise later in the season.
> − Neglect slug and snail monitoring as growth begins.
> − Remove spring bulb foliage before it yellows naturally.

dead growth. Start hardening off protected plants gradually (see Step 6 on p.41). Also think about slug and snail management before populations explode, monitoring the mollusc emergence as temperatures warm, and using your chosen methods of keeping them from treasured plants. For me, that means copper ring guards, nematodes and the occasional moonlight slug hunt.

Strategic Pruning

Tackle late-summer flowering shrubs such as buddleia and *Caryopteris* or the winter stems of dogwood (*Cornus*), cutting back hard to encourage vigorous growth. Begin rose maintenance, too, removing dead, diseased or crossing wood, then reducing stems by about a third. Leave spring-flowering shrubs that bloom on the previous year's growth – wait until after flowering before pruning these.

Early Spring

Creating Walls of Colour
Pruning and training established climbers

I have a confession to make – I always put off pruning and tying in my roses until new growth emerges. This isn't what books tell you to do; they'd prefer you did it from late autumn through to winter, but it's hard to get to the back of full borders at that time of year and not an attractive option in the cold. So, I wait. As the sap rises, so does my motivation to train my climbers' vertical growth to maximise future colour.

1 Assess before you attack
Study your climbers on a bright morning. Consider their shape and the directions you would like them to grow. For clematis, check which group it belongs to (1, 2 or 3) before making a single cut, or you might accidentally remove this season's flowers!

2 Gather the right tools
Sharp, clean secateurs make all the difference between a good cut and a messy tear. I've learnt through bitter experience that blunt tools lead to disease entry points. Use loppers for thicker stems, and for woody climbers, a small pruning saw is essential. Don't forget sturdy gloves – my battle-scarred hands are testament to rose thorns that penetrate even 'thornproof' gloves.

3 Start with the obvious cuts
Begin by removing anything dead, diseased or damaged. On roses, check for brown pith inside dead-looking stems with small test cuts; this is a sign of die back and you should remove any, but leave those with green or white centres. Also take out the oldest, woodiest stems which will be less productive than the new. With clematis, brittle, hollow stems won't recover and should go. Be ruthless – every snip redirects energy toward new growth.

4 Shape for maximum flower power
Train climbers horizontally or in gentle curves rather than vertically. This slows sap flow, forcing more flowering points. For climbing roses, identify 5–7 strong framework branches to fan out, then prune side shoots to 2–3 buds.

5 Train deliberately
Attach plant stems in patterns that maximise coverage rather than allowing vertical growth alone. Use soft twine, tying it in a figure-of-eight for delicate growth, and use two strands of twine for mature stems. The key is securing without strangling them – strangulated plants produce fewer flowers and shorter displays. Leave room, too, for natural swelling as stems thicken through the growing season.

6 Feed for colour intensity
Once structural work is complete, feed your climbers appropriately for their type – roses benefit from a balanced fertiliser, clematis prefers potassium-rich feeds. Apply a generous 5cm (2in) layer of mulch – good home-made compost or well-rotted manure, keeping it clear of the base to prevent crown rot. Both will increase the flowering you've encouraged through pruning, ensuring a productive season ahead.

Kitchen Table Seed Sowing

My obsession for extra colour is easily-satisfied with seeds

My treasured old seed tin holds hundreds of possibilities for summer displays. Early spring's lengthening days awaken germination potential just when I'm craving colour the most. Sowing seeds lets you grow plants that transform your garden into personal, kaleidoscopic colour symphonies of your own making, and the possibilities are endless.

1 Design your colour scheme
Before opening a single packet, plan your summer colour display. I organise seeds by colour and flowering time, ensuring waves of coordinated blooms. Select quick growers such as calendula alongside slower developers like cosmos, and note germination times. This staggered approach delivers non-stop colour from early summer to late autumn.

2 Commandeer your growing space
You don't need a greenhouse for successful seed sowing. My table-top becomes mission control each spring, with a heated propagator for warmth-lovers and tiered shelving maximising limited space, positioned where I can see emerging seedlings. While fancy equipment helps, simple recycled containers work brilliantly for colour-rich annuals such as sunflowers and nasturtiums. What matters is light quality – position near windows or under grow lights to prevent legginess.

3 Get the basics right
Quality compost creates healthy plants that flower prolifically. I use peat-free mixes that hold moisture without waterlogging. Fill containers to just below the rim, then create a perfectly level surface that ensures even germination.

4 Sow with self-control
The greatest seed-sowing mistake? Grabbing seed packets and sowing them all. We want a succession of growth that produces fresh flowers continuously, rather than one big but quickly exhausted display. Sow in small batches as the season progresses.

5 Master watering
Technique dramatically affects final plant quality. For freshly sown seeds, use a fine mist spray rather than a watering can, which displaces tiny seeds. Once germinated, water from below by filling trays beneath pots – this keeps foliage dry, helping to prevent fungal issues.

6 Graduate to garden life
As seedlings develop true leaves, prick them out and pot each on into individual pots or modules, before beginning the crucial hardening off process. Start when overnight temperatures become reliably mild, gradually increasing outdoor exposure by setting them outside during the day for a week or two and bringing them indoors at night. This strengthens stems. Pinch out growing tips of branching annuals such as cosmos and salvias when they reach 20–30cm (8–12in) – this simple action transforms single stems into multi-flowered plants.

Late Spring

Can you feel the change? Late spring strides in with purposeful determination, bringing with it a strengthening light that further coaxes gardens from their winter slumber. Ferns unfurl their feathery fronds, the freshest flecks of green emerge on tree branches, and scent swirls through the air, drifting from tiny lily of the valley blooms and erupting from lilacs. Bees buzz close to collect nectar and pollen, sometimes dozing in the gentle cradle of a flower, lulled by the sun's warmth. After months of looking at bare soil and leafless stems, this transformation feels nothing short of miraculous.

The garden now becomes a kaleidoscope of colours, textures and forms – after long months of short daylight hours, these riotous hues are a delight. With the baton passing from daffodils to tulips, which boldly stride into the light with their saturated shades, spring's crescendo is well underway. *Fritillaria imperialis* and *Camassia* step forward to take centre stage, their architectural forms adding vertical drama to the sudden abundance.

As the garden begins to swell, I find myself practically itching to get my hands dirty. Gone are the days of trudging out in wellies and woollies – it's time to shed some layers and put on the sunglasses, with only sunscreen as a permanent fixture in my gardening garb. Tending to our garden's needs transforms from an 'I must do this' chore to an 'I can't wait to get out there' everyday pleasure.

This seasonal pivot point is when I focus on designing for colour impact. My palette for late spring centres around jewel tones that complement the fresh green backdrop – rich purples, deep blues, and splashes of bright pinks and yellows create a tapestry that sings with vitality. I'm drawn to the indigo spires of *Camassia leichtlinii* subsp. *suksdorfii* Caerulea Group, which rise

Late spring at its best – orange and purple tulips in a mix of pots bringing pure joy to the garden (and the gardener!)

like slender sentinels through emerging perennials, and the regal purple globes of *Allium hollandicum* 'Purple Sensation' that add punctuation marks of colour throughout the borders. The voluptuous forms of iris, be they Benton or otherwise, bring a sophisticated elegance that feels perfectly timed for this moment in the year.

For memorable planting combinations, I pair my irises with the acid yellow flowers of *Euphorbia amygdaloides* var. *robbiae* and pure white cups of *Narcissus* 'Thalia'. There's something about this contrast between cool and warm tones that creates a dynamic tension, bringing borders to life in a way that more obvious combinations sometimes fail to achieve. Beneath these stars, I thread the frothy white flowers of *Anthriscus sylvestris* 'Ravenswing', its deep chocolate stems and feathery foliage adding a layer of sophistication that grounds the more flamboyant blooms above.

Every leading actor needs a strong supporting cast, and late spring's showstoppers are no exception. The fresh, lime-green foliage of emerging perennials such as *Alchemilla mollis* and *Tellima grandiflora* provides the perfect backdrop to more dramatic blooms, their leaves catching morning dew in perfect crystalline droplets. Ferns come into their own now, too – I watch with fascination as the emerging croziers of the ostrich fern (*Matteuccia struthiopteris*) unfurl with prehistoric precision in the freshest green, while the furry fronds of *Polystichum setiferum* 'Herrenhausen' add textural complexity that makes the garden feel more three-dimensional, inviting you to reach out and touch.

Rhododendron luteum holds court above my husband's much treasured box balls – late spring's perfect partnership of wild exuberance meeting clipped precision, adding warmth to the shade

Tulips catch the light **(left)**; while ferns unfurl towards the same sun, all among self-seeded *Lunaria annua* 'Chedglow' **(right)**

If you have a smaller city garden, take advantage of this time of year by thinking strategically – space may be limited, but there's always room to grow in pots, or upwards. Position tulips in containers carefully to create focal points that draw the eye. Amelanchiers lift borders with their gift of blowsy flowers that lead your gaze to the sky, and climbing *Clematis alpina* or *C. macropetala* in varieties that suit your colour scheme stitch their way across fence panels and up buildings to soften your space.

Container displays take on new importance, offering seasonal showcases that can be appreciated up close. I layer bulbs in autumn for a sequential display that peaks now – early-flowering varieties provide the first flush of colour, followed by mid-season performers, with late-flowering options extending the show into early summer. The bolder the better. From the rich blackberry multi-headed blooms of *Tulipa* 'Havran' to the tonal oranges of 'Apricot Foxx', they create a fiery progression that evolves over weeks, telling a story of the season's advance.

   The approach shifts when working with larger country gardens, where the scale allows for more sweeping gestures. Perennial tulips – such as the Darwin hybrids ('Banja Luka' is a great mixer), Fosteriana and species such as *Tulipa tarda*, *T. clusiana* and *T. sylvestris* planted in large, irregular groups in the ground are the order of the day. More demure, the snake's head fritillary (*Fritillaria meleagris*) spreading through grass creates a meadow-like effect that feels both sophisticated and wild. As spring breezes move through, their nodding heads create a gentle ballet, catching light and shadow in ways that change throughout the day. Despite their delicate appearance, these fritillaries are surprisingly tough, thriving in various soil conditions and self-seeding when happy.
   Anemone 'Mr Fokker' is another showstopper I can't resist – characterful, charming, and with a certain sophistication, its crosses the divide between early and late spring with its deep blue blooms that never fail to make me smile, whether planted in pots, borders or meadows.

Container displays in full bloom offer pure contentment in late spring – a wonderful time for gardening, when it's warm enough to work comfortably, but cool enough to keep going

There's something almost magical about seeing light filter through the fine hairs on a leaf's edge or illuminate the intricate structure of a grass flower

As the season progresses, texture becomes increasingly important – the soft, fuzzy leaves of emerging *Stachys byzantina* 'Purple Rain' contrast beautifully with the tousled hairy clumps of grasses such as *Deschampsia cespitosa*. I've learned to position these textural players where afternoon light will backlight them, enhancing their tactile qualities and adding another dimension to the garden's visual appeal. There's something almost magical about seeing light filter through the fine hairs on a leaf's edge or illuminate the intricate structure of a grass flower.

Late spring also prompts me to think ahead, considering the transition into early summer and how to make it seamless. I interplant late-spring performers with those that will take over as the seasons advance. The airy, white umbels of *Cenolophium denudatum* rise above emerging perennials, as does fennel (*Foeniculum vulgare*), bridging the seasonal gap with their delicate presence. These transparent plants create a gauzy layer that softens transitions between more structural elements, lending the garden a sense of depth and mystery.

When designing late spring colour schemes, I'm mindful of creating moments of surprise and delight – a pocket of intense colour glimpsed through an archway, or a fragrant plant positioned near a path where its scent can be fully appreciated. These thoughtful touches transform a garden from merely pretty to truly memorable, creating experiences rather than just views.

Late spring embodies promise and potential – it's the moment when the garden's full personality begins to emerge once more. It's also the time to begin sowing seed in earnest, with colour, texture and form in mind, to fill gaps, pots and your garden to create a place that not only looks beautiful but feels alive with possibility.

Spring's Zesty Awakening

Perennial tulips dance with emerging foliage

Viridiflora tulips are a gardener's dream, reducing the need for annual planting, as unlike many hybrid tulips, these perennials return year after year. The bulbs are an excellent investment for your garden and a relief for your back!

Each year, I eagerly await the zesty spring border combination these tulips create. Viridifloras stand out from others in the tulip family with their distinctive, green-streaked petals in various hues. I favour a warm orange mixed with vibrant yellow, both striking against the lush backdrop of my woodland-edge front garden borders.

The stars of the show for me are 'Orange Marmalade' and 'Green Mile'. Their supporting cast includes the elegant white *Narcissus* 'Thalia' and cheerful 'Regeneration', which bloom slightly earlier to announce the tulips' grand entrance. This combination, complemented by a backdrop of flowering *Cornus kousa* and rhododendrons, offers a spectacular display that evolves beautifully from early to late spring, and with zero effort from me, too.

Tulipa **'Orange Marmalade'** This Viridiflora tulip's striking orange petals with green flames create an out-of-the-ordinary effect, and return reliably year after year, multiplying slowly over time. Deadhead after flowering, but allow foliage to die back naturally. **HARDINESS: RHS H6**

Tulipa **'Green Mile'** Another Viridiflora tulip, the elegant green flowers with yellow edges are a sophisticated companion to 'Orange Marmalade'. Excellent as cut flowers, long-lasting in vases, they are also remarkably resistant to deer and rodents. Plant in groups of 7–9 for maximum impact. **HARDINESS: RHS H6**

Narcissus **'Thalia'** This daffodil's graceful white flowers, 2–3 per stem, offer a pure, elegant contrast and naturalise well in grass or woodland settings. A low-maintenance bulb; allow the foliage to die back naturally to feed next year's blooms. **HARDINESS: RHS H6**

Narcissus **'Regeneration'** Cheerful yellow flowers with slightly ruffled cups bring a burst of sunshine to the spring garden, while the fragrant blooms are excellent for cutting. This daffodil multiplies readily over time, forming large clumps. Plant in drifts for a natural look. **HARDINESS: RHS H6**

> **TIPS FOR SUCCESS**
> - Plant the bulbs in autumn, 15–20cm (6–8in) deep in well-drained soil.
> - Apply a balanced fertiliser when new growth emerges.
> - Deadhead spent blooms promptly.
> - Allow foliage to die back naturally after flowering.
> - Lift and divide tulip bulbs every 3–4 years to prevent overcrowding.
> - Apply well-rotted compost as mulch in late autumn.

Tulipa 'Orange Marmalade' **(top left)**; *Narcissus* 'Regeneration' **(top right)**; the full combination in vivid display **(bottom)**

Nature's Origami

The unfolding of shade's perennial powerhouses

As late spring ushers in warmer days, the shade garden awakens with its display of textures and colours. Perennials emerge to take centre stage, helpfully concealing the daffodils' fading bulb foliage. For me, the undisputed highlight of this vernal stirring is the unfurling of the ferns – a mesmerizing process, as tightly coiled fiddleheads stretch out like octopus tentacles, intertwining with neighbouring plants.

The native soft shield fern *Polystichum setiferum* 'Herrenhausen' stands out, with its rough, chestnut-leaf texture, while *Epimedium × perralchicum* 'Fröhnleiten' offers glossy, bronze-russet hearts and delicate yellow blooms as a contrast. These tough evergreens are workhorses, thriving even in dry, tree-root-laden soil, creating a lush understory that transforms shaded spaces into vibrant, textured wonderlands.

Polystichum setiferum **(Divisilobum Group) 'Herrenhausen'** The elegant soft shield fern brings year-round texture to shady borders with its robust fronds. Thriving in full shade and dry, tree-root-heavy soil, it's ideal for challenging spots. Slow-growing and low-maintenance, it is deer-resistant, too. **HARDINESS: RHS H7**

Epimedium × perralchicum **'Fröhnleiten'** Heart-shaped leaves emerge bronze, maturing to glossy green, while delicate yellow 'fairy wing' flowers bloom in mid-spring. Excellent under deciduous trees, where summer drought is an issue. this versatile ground-cover perennial thrives in dry shade, spreading without being invasive. Trim old foliage in late winter to encourage spring's colourful young growth. **HARDINESS: RHS H6**

TIPS FOR SUCCESS

- Mulch *Polystichum* in early spring to maintain soil moisture.
- Remove dead fronds from *Polystichum* in spring for year-round beauty.
- Water *Epimedium* deeply during extended dry periods.
- Both plants tolerate dry shade once established.
- Group with other shade-lovers for a rich, layered look.

Close-up of *Polystichum setiferum* (Divisilobum Group) 'Herrenhausen' **(right)**; *Epimedium × perralchicum* 'Fröhnleiten' **(opposite)**

Late Spring

Layers of Luxe

The thrill of the tulip lasagne for container gardens

After winter's short, cold days, I crave bold colour. A potted tulip lasagne brings a kaleidoscopic spectacle of shapes and heights unmatched by other spring bulb displays. Perfect for sun-drenched patios, doorsteps or balconies, this layered technique creates an explosion of colour and texture lasting many weeks, enhanced by grouping containers of various shapes and sizes (see also p.166 for instructions).

Here, deep purples and maroons ignite with vibrant oranges, shouting 'spring is here', with an added luminous glow when backlit by the sun. Dark, velvety 'Slawa' tulips emerge first, followed by bright 'Apricot Foxx', then the warm sunset hues of 'Cairo' and 'Synaeda Orange', until the rich, dramatic tones of 'Continental' finally emerge.

For an unexpected touch, I add blue *Anemone coronaria* (De Caen Group) 'Mister Fokker', a cool counterpoint, cutting through the warm tones. If these begin to dominate, they can be cut for indoor vases – a win-win indeed!

> **TIPS FOR SUCCESS**
> - Keep the compost moist during the growth period; reduce watering after flowering.
> - Apply a balanced fertiliser when planting, and then a high potassium type after blooming.
> - Line terracotta pots with old compost bags, punching it with holes at the bottom, to keep the containers cool and moist.
> - Use fresh bulbs and a well-draining peat-free compost mix to prevent the fungal disease, tulip fire.

Tulipa **'Apricot Foxx'** This Darwin Hybrid tulip features soft apricot petals blushed with pink, its large, goblet-shaped blooms opening wide in the sun. Plant in the bottom layer for late-season colour. It's excellent for cutting, too. **HARDINESS: RHS H6**

Tulipa **'Cairo'** A single late tulip with deep burgundy petals and golden-orange edges. The tall stems are ideal for the back of container displays or as dramatic cut flowers. Plant in the bottom layer for late-spring blooms. **HARDINESS: RHS H6**

Tulipa **'Slawa'** The deep maroon petals edged in warm amber of this statuesque tulip pair beautifully with orange and apricot varieties, creating a rich, sophisticated palette. Plant in the middle layer for mid-season drama. **HARDINESS: RHS H6**

Tulipa **'Synaeda Orange'** A Triumph tulip boasting vibrant orange blooms with subtle yellow bases, with strong stems that resist flopping in rainy weather. It combines well with purples and deep reds. Plant in the middle layer for mid-season impact. **HARDINESS: RHS H6**

Tulipa **'Continental'** The deep maroon flowers of this single early tulip create a rich, dramatic look. It provides a bold foundation in container displays, supporting more vibrant hues. Plant in the top layer for early-season flowers. **HARDINESS: RHS H6**

Anemone coronaria **(De Caen Group) 'Mister Fokker'** Vivid blue, poppy-like flowers that grow to 20–30cm (8–12in), adding cool contrast to warm-toned tulips. Plant corms in autumn or early spring in the top layer. **HARDINESS: RHS H5**

Tulipa 'Cairo' and *Tulipa* 'Slawa' speaking the same colour language

New blooms open as others fade – the brilliance of planting tulips in layers means the show just keeps on coming

Opposite *Tulipa* 'Continental' dancing above bright companions – late spring's lesson in colour contrast

Above *Anemone* 'Mister Fokker' gatecrashing the tulip party Those papery blue petals know how to make an entrance

Yellow Fantasy

Unexpected sunshine for shady spots

The sunny firework displays of *Allium* 'Yellow Fantasy' bring unexpected brightness to this foliage combination, their cheerful chartreuse spheres dancing above a tapestry of varied leaf textures. The soft, pleated fans of *Alchemilla mollis* provide a gentle backdrop, while the intricate, lacy fronds of *Briza minor* add architectural elegance. Beneath, the heart-shaped leaves of *Epimedium × perralchicum* 'Fröhnleiten' create a bronze-tinged carpet that extends through the seasons.

This combination thrives in partial shade with moisture-retentive, well-drained soil, making it perfect for woodland edges. The display peaks in late spring when the alliums bloom but continues to provide interest through summer with the contrasting foliage textures. For sunnier spots, substitute *Alchemilla* with *Heuchera* varieties, or add *Brunnera macrophylla* 'Jack Frost' for additional silver-splashed leaves if you've got very deep shade.

Allium **'Yellow Fantasy'** This unusual, gorgeous spring bulb produces delicate balls of flower in bright chartreuse-yellow florets on 35cm (1ft) stems. Blooming in late spring, it brings unexpected sunshine to shaded areas where most alliums struggle. Plant bulbs in autumn in well-drained soil and allow foliage to die back naturally to feed next year's display.
HARDINESS: RHS H5–6

Alchemilla mollis The soft, scalloped leaves of lady's mantle catch the morning dew beautifully, creating a sparkling effect long before the tiny chartreuse flowers appear in early summer. Cut back hard after flowering to encourage fresh foliage. This perennial self-seeds readily; deadhead to control spread if desired. **HARDINESS: RHS H7**

Briza minor This soft shield fern produces deeply divided, lacy fronds that create intricate patterns of light and shadow. Growing to 60cm (2ft) tall, it provides year-round structure and architectural interest. Prefers humus-rich, well-drained soil in shade to partial shade, and benefits from sheltered positions.
HARDINESS: RHS H7

***Epimedium × perralchicum* 'Fröhnleiten'**
(see p.53)

TIPS FOR SUCCESS

- Set allium bulbs at three times their depth in autumn, adding grit to the bottom of your planting hole in heavy soils to prevent rotting during winter months.
- Apply leaf mould or well-rotted compost around plants each spring to maintain moisture and improve soil structure for optimal growth.
- Trim *Alchemilla* flower stems and foliage after blooming to prevent excessive self-seeding and encouraging regrowth.
- Divide *Epimedium* clumps every 4–5 years in early spring before new growth begins to rejuvenate and expand the planting.
- Remove old *Polystichum* fronds in late winter before new growth unfurls.

Deep Drama

Bold burgundy leaves anchoring ethereal spires

The elegant spires of *Camassia leichtlinii* subsp. *suksdorfii* Caerulea Group create a breathtaking contrast against the deeply textured, bronze-burgundy foliage of *Rodgersia podophylla* 'Braunlaub'. This sophisticated pairing demonstrates how foliage can provide the perfect stage for delicate flowers, with the *Rodgersia*'s architectural, palm-like leaves creating dramatic shadows and depth while the *Camassia*'s star-shaped blooms dance on slender stems above.

This combination thrives in partial shade with consistently moist, humus-rich soil, making it ideal for woodland gardens or bog garden edges. The display peaks in late spring when the *Camassia* blooms, but the *Rodgersia*'s striking foliage provides interest throughout the growing season, changing to green before again developing richer bronze tones as summer progresses.

***Camassia leichtlinii* subsp. *suksdorfii* Caerulea Group** This North American native bulb produces tall spires of star-shaped, clear blue flowers reaching 80–120cm (2⅗–4ft) in late spring. The flowers open progressively up the stem, extending the display over several weeks. Plant bulbs in autumn in moisture-retentive soil, allowing foliage to die back naturally. Excellent for naturalising and beloved by pollinators. **HARDINESS: RHS H4**

***Rodgersia podophylla* 'Braunlaub'**
A magnificent architectural perennial with large, palmate leaves that emerge rich bronze-burgundy, providing dramatic foliage interest throughout the season. Reaching 90cm (3ft) tall, it produces creamy-white flower plumes in summer, though it's primarily grown for its stunning leaf display. Requires consistently moist soil and shelter from strong winds that can damage the large leaves. **HARDINESS: RHS H6**

> **TIPS FOR SUCCESS**
> - Ensure consistent soil moisture, especially during dry spells, as both plants suffer in drought conditions and leaves may scorch.
> - Plant *Camassia* bulbs 10–15cm (4–6in) deep in autumn, adding organic matter to improve soil structure and moisture retention.
> - Position *Rodgersia* in sheltered spots to prevent wind damage to the large, architectural leaves which can tear easily.
> - Apply a thick layer of organic mulch around plants each spring to retain moisture and suppress competing weeds.
> - Divide *Rodgersia* clumps every 4–5 years in early spring when dormant, ensuring each section has good root development.

WHAT TO DO
LATE SPRING

Late spring is a crucial time in the garden, and there's a multitude of tasks to keep us gardeners busy. From sowing and planting to pruning and maintaining your tools, the work you put in during this season lays the foundation for stunning displays later in the year. So, roll up your sleeves, grab your kneeler and find the twine – at last we can get out there and garden!

Essential tools

As the weather warms up and plants burst into life in late spring, having the right tools at the ready is essential for efficient gardening, ensuring you don't get distracted as you trudge back to your shed to get what you need. I like to be prepared, keeping my secateurs and hori-hori in holsters on my belt, ready for action, kind of like a horticultural cowgirl!

Secateurs are indispensable for pruning spring-flowering shrubs, deadheading spent blooms and harvesting early crops, while a hori-hori, a versatile Japanese gardening knife, is perfect for weeding, planting and dividing overcrowded perennials. Before I step outside, I've trained myself to give my tools a quick clean and sharpen. It's now become a habit, keeping them ready to make those clean cuts that allow plants to heal quickly and reduce the risk of infection.

I also make sure I have a generous pocketful of twine, cut to length, ready to tie in any plants that need support – usually wayward perennials or catapulting climbers – dealing with them quickly and efficiently so neither get damaged through neglect.

Remember, a sharp, clean tool makes for a happy gardener, and by keeping your arsenal at your hip, you're always ready to tackle whatever late spring throws at you.

Timely Staking

As the last petals of tulips and daffodils fade and flutter to the ground, it's your cue to start staking those emerging tall, top-heavy or floppy perennials, reducing the risk of damage from late spring storms or the weight of upcoming summer blooms. Staking now means there's still space in your borders to get to them and your top-heavy beauties are small enough to prevent an undignified fall in the wind or weather.

Bamboo canes, wooden stakes or metal supports are all popular choices, but remember, we're aiming for subtle support that's easy on the eye, encourages more natural, graceful growth, and doesn't encage the plant, which in itself can be damaging.

Gently insert your support close to the base of the plant, taking care not to damage its delicate root system. Use soft, flexible ties, such as twine or plant ties, if necessary, to secure the plant at regular intervals, using the figure-of-eight knot outlined on p.64. Avoid tying too tightly or too loosely, and check regularly as the seasons progress to see if your twine needs replacing or if the knot needs to be loosened.

Mastering the Figure-of-Eight Knot

As late spring arrives, climbing plants such as clematis, jasmine and honeysuckle begin their enthusiastic seasonal ascent. The figure-of-eight knot is a gardener's best friend for these plants, guiding climbers into position in the direction you'd like them to grow and providing secure support without damaging delicate stems.

Start with a length of twine and create a loop around the plant stem, leaving enough slack for growth. Pass one end of the twine over the other, and tie the ends behind the support structure to create a figure-of-eight shape. Gently tighten, then make a knot, ensuring that it is snug but not constricting, before trimming off any excess twine to keep things neat.

Lift and Divide

Late spring is an ideal time to breathe new life into overcrowded perennials to keep them healthy and more floriferous, with the added bonus of providing you with plants for free. As the soil warms up and plants awaken, many of our perennial stalwarts are growing at a rate of knots and can be divided into smaller clumps.

Begin by giving the plant you've chosen to divide a good drink of water the day before. Then, using a garden spade, carefully slice into the soil, forming a circle around the plant, before lifting the entire clump from the ground, taking care to preserve as much of the root system as possible. Gently shake to allow excess soil to fall away to reveal the root structure. Use the spade, or a sharp, clean knife (an old bread knife or pruning saw is ideal) to divide the clump into smaller sections, each containing a healthy portion of roots and leafy stems. Be ruthless with any dead, diseased or woody parts – they're best removed to your compost bin, along with any tall top growth, which will inevitably slump after transplanting.

Replant the divisions as soon as possible, ensuring they are at the same depth in the ground or their new pot as the original plant was in the soil. A good watering and a layer of mulch will help settle them into their new homes.

Direct Sowing

As the frosts begin to fade into memory, late spring invites you to direct sow hardy annual seeds. It's a wonderfully simple, quick and cost-effective way to inject colour into your garden, just as the soil is warming up, without having to arduously prick out and pot on germinated seedlings when there's already much to do. Hardy annuals are perfect for this method: they're tough, fast-growing plants with a robust nature that allows them to survive late spring's variable weather.

Before you begin, take a moment to look over your borders and hoe off any emerging weeds that are making their home in your annuals' territory. Next, prepare the soil by raking it to a fine, breadcrumb texture, checking the seed packet for specific sowing instructions, as each species may have different requirements.

Many popular hardy annuals for late spring sowing, including cornflowers, poppies, marigolds and zinnias, are eager to please and can be scattered in rows, then gently raked in. For tiny seeds, mixing them with sand can make sprinkling easier. Another tip is to sow them in diagonal lines across your planting bed for a more naturalistic look. Either way, label the rows with the variety and date so you can distinguish them from opportunistic weeds which will grow up around them.

A gentle watering with a fine spray will settle them in without washing them away, then keep the soil moist as you await the magical moment of germination. Once the seedlings have developed their first set of true leaves, thin them out to prevent overcrowding and give each plant room to flourish.

Though direct sowing doesn't give you the same level of control as growing annual plants in pots or module trays, it's fun and simple, allowing you to create vibrant, informal displays that not only delight the eye but attract a host of pollinators to your garden, too. What could be more joyful than that?

MY ESSENTIAL DOS AND DON'TS

+ Sow hardy annuals directly into the ground to bring a burst of summer colour.
+ Plant out hardy summer annuals alongside container-grown perennial plants to fill gaps in borders and to fill garden pots.
+ Deadhead spring-flowering bulbs and perennials to encourage more blooms.
+ Prune spring-flowering shrubs after they've finished blooming to maintain their shape.
+ Stake tall perennials and climbing plants to provide support and prevent wind damage.
+ Water new plants regularly.
+ Apply a layer of mulch around plants to retain moisture and suppress weeds.
+ Start hardening off tender plants before planting them outdoors (see Step 6 on p.41).
+ Mow lawns regularly and apply a spring lawn fertiliser.

− Plant tender annuals or heat-loving vegetables outdoors until the risk of frost has passed.
− Overwater established plants, as this can lead to root rot and fungal issues.
− Let weeds go to seed, making them harder to control later on.
− Cut back spring-flowering bulb foliage until it has turned yellow and died back.
− Neglect container plants; ensure they receive regular watering and feeding.
− Use pesticides as they harm beneficial insects.
− Let perennials become too crowded; divide them if need be to maintain health.

Late Spring

Mind the Gap
Plug gaps now for full summer borders

Did you notice gaps in your border last summer? Now's the time to check last year's garden photographs or notebooks and plug them. This allows you to strategically place blooms where you need them most, brightening up the months when your garden is low on colour, and ensuring a seamless transition from spring to summer, and on into autumn and winter.

1 Assess your border gaps and keep records
Take note of any gaps that appear in your garden borders throughout the year. Back these up with photographs to help you remember the location, size and surrounding plants.

2 Mark gaps with bamboo canes or sticks
As you identify gaps, place canes or sticks in the spaces. This is a brilliant visual cue, reminding you where you need to add plants and also making sure that your new plant purchases are appropriate for the site.

3 Choose your new plants
Carefully select your new plants, thinking about colour, foliage, texture, shape and size, ensuring your choices complement the existing plants around them, without crowding them. Also make sure new purchases are suitable for your soil type and the aspect.

Buy at least three of each new variety to prevent your borders from feeling overly fussy. Or you could buy one large pot of perennials and split the plants in it, which is better environmentally and usually saves money.

To check plants are healthy and well-established, take them out of their pot at the garden centre or nursery, to check they're not pot-bound.

4 Prepare the planting area
Clear any weeds from the gaps in your border, then use a garden fork or trowel to loosen the soil to a depth of about 20–25cm (8–10in). This will help the roots establish quickly. If your soil is poor, incorporate some well-rotted compost or organic matter to improve its structure and fertility.

5 Plant your containerised plants
Remove each plant from its container by gently squeezing the sides and tipping it out. If the roots are tightly coiled, tease them out gently to encourage them to grow outwards. Dig a hole in your border slightly larger than the root ball of your plant. Place the plant in the hole, ensuring that it sits at the same depth as it did in its container. Backfill with soil and firm gently around the base.

6 Water and mulch
After planting, give your new additions a thorough watering. Apply a layer of mulch, such as fine composted bark chips or compost, around the base of each plant to help retain moisture, suppress weeds, and regulate soil temperature. Keep the mulch a few centimetres away from the plant stems to prevent rot. Water your newly planted additions regularly, especially during dry spells.

Potted pelargoniums

Create a fresh, fragrant table display to enjoy all summer long

Planting pelargoniums in terracotta pots in late spring is a great way to plan for vibrant summer colour later in the year. There's nothing more enjoyable than browsing specialist nurseries online, daydreaming about the sights and scents promised by these easy-to-grow plants, and it is the perfect excuse to buy more plants which emulate the warmth and light of future days in the sun. Let's explore the process of potting up these beauties step by step.

1 Match varieties to pot sizes
Pelargoniums thrive in terracotta pots, which provide excellent drainage, allowing excess moisture to evaporate and the roots to breathe, reducing the risk of root rot. Check the eventual height and spread of the varieties you've chosen and match with an appropriate pot size. As an aside, always ensure each container has drainage holes to prevent waterlogging, which pelargoniums detest.

2 Prepare your pots
Before planting, add a layer of crocks or gravel to the bottom of each pot. Fill the pots with a high-quality, peat-free compost, leaving space for the plant.

3 Position and plant your pelargoniums
Place each pelargonium, still in its nursery pot, into the terracotta pot to gauge the planting depth – the plant stems should all be above the compost surface. This allows you to make adjustments without damaging the roots. Then, carefully remove the plant from its nursery pot and place it into the gap. Gently firm the compost around the plant, ensuring good contact between the roots and soil.

4 Add a layer of horticultural grit
After planting, add a layer of horticultural grit on top of the compost. This helps retain moisture in the soil and prevents water from splashing on to the foliage, which can lead to fungal diseases. It also adds a decorative touch!

5 Label your pots and display them
Label each pot with the variety name and planting date. This will act as a helpful reminder for the future, and help you provide the appropriate care. Once all your pots are planted and labelled (the more the merrier in my opinion!), then group them together as I do on my large oak garden table. Displaying them at varying heights creates a visually appealing and impactful arrangement.

6 Water and feed
When the top couple of centimetres of compost in your pots feels dry, reach for the watering can and give them a soak. Always water at the base of the plant to prevent fungal disease and allow the top of the compost to dry out between waterings. Feed with a light liquid feed once every two weeks.

Early Summer

Early summer arrives in a crescendo of colour and fragrance, sweeping away spring with bold, saturated hues. The garden begins to build to a magnificent peak of abundance – trees and shrubs are fully clothed in leaf, climbers unfurl their perfect petals in quick succession, while herbaceous perennials surge upward with seemingly unstoppable energy, often overnight! The light feels different too – clear, strong and hard, lingering late into evenings that smell of honeysuckle and freshly cut grass.

This is the season when gardens hit their stride, fulfilling their promise. After months of planning, planting and patient anticipation, we're rewarded with a spectacular display that changes daily. I find myself skipping around the garden each morning with eager eyes and a stroking hand, noticing what's newly opened, colour combinations that are working particularly well, and which plants are preparing to take their turn as my new favourites. There's something awe-inspiring about this time of year – it feels expansive and generous, as if the garden is showing off everything it can do, all at once.

The intensity of growth can be almost overwhelming, with each plant seeming determined to outdo its neighbours in height, spread and floriferousness – exactly what makes early summer so thrilling. It's nature in supercharge mode, bursting with vitality and demanding our attention. The garden hums with life, too – bees zigzag between flowers, butterflies perform aerial acrobatics above borders and birds busy themselves with second broods amid treetop roosts.

I adore all of the exuberance and devour the colour greedily. My early summer palette centres on fiery yellow topaz, ruby reds and amethyst purples – balancing this kaleidoscopic colour with

Early summer's exuberance – every plant racing to outdo its neighbours, borders humming with life and colour at every level

buffers of foliage produced by perennials that will bloom later in the season, this leafy layer helping to prevent the overall effect from becoming too overwhelming. Now is the moment for bold statements and dramatic combinations that might feel excessive in other seasons but in early summer seem perfectly in tune with the garden and our moods.

For many, roses naturally take centre stage, their perfect blooms and intoxicating scent epitomising everything we love about summer gardens. Rather than isolating them in dedicated beds, with limited space, I knit them up the walls of our house and through the borders, where they oomph among billowing perennials, and offer a welcome when I return home. *Rosa* THE SIMPLE LIFE, with her open, single, peach-pink, long-flowering blooms offers the simplicity of a dog rose and wonderful winter hips to admire as I reach for the key to my front door. In the borders, *Rosa × odorata* 'Mutabilis' is a wonderful warm mixer, with its vibrant blooms that change from pale yellow to pink and finally to a deep crimson colour, all on the same plant.

For reliable flower power, I opt for early-blooming hardy geraniums such as *Geranium* PATRICIA, whose cerise-pink flowers jostle through and among her border peers for months without pause. Indeed, almost all members of the geranium family, in whichever colour you choose, provide vigorous perennials that weave through borders, filling gaps and creating cohesion between more structural plants. I wouldn't be without them in any garden I design.

The transparent qualities of certain plants become particularly valuable now. The airy flower heads of *Stipa gigantea* catch the light beautifully, adding movement and a golden sheen to borders, quietening *Helenium* 'Moerheim Beauty' and other,

Bolder colours take over everywhere you look – *Veronicastrum* **(top left)**, *Helenium* **(top right)** and *Crocosmia* **(bottom)** making sure early summer can't be ignored from any angle

bolder counterparts. *Verbena bonariensis*, with its slender stems topped with small purple flowers, appears to float above lower-growing plants, creating a see-through layer that adds depth, without blocking views of plants behind. Similarly, out front, the delicate umbels of *Cenolophium denudatum* create a gauzy white layer that softens transitions between more substantial plants.

In my own garden, I've punctuated an early summer border with the rich purple globes of *Allium* 'Summer Drummer', which rise through a sea of salvias and *Echinacea*, the flowers hovering, almost unfeasibly, above an array of bold beauties. As the allium flowers fade, their structural seed heads continue to add interest well into late summer, quiet observers as the garden reaches its crescendo. These architectural elements provide a framework that supports the more ephemeral blooms, creating a garden that evolves rather than peaks and fades.

For those with extensive country gardens, I find that almost anything goes, but careful planning still yields the most satisfying results. My penchant is for *Geum* 'Totally Tangerine' mixed with its cousin G. SCARLET TEMPEST, the technicolour daisies supported by the upright forms of salvias, if not *Salvia nemorosa* 'Caradonna', then 'Amethyst'. In these larger spaces, I design where bold colours, textures and ecology converge to create captivating natural havens to stimulate all the senses – sight, touch, sound, taste and smell – and bringing nature within reach.

In smaller gardens, I focus on creating layers that maximise impact in limited space. A carefully positioned small tree like

Betonica officinalis 'Hummelo' doing what it does best – providing weeks of purple punch that carries early summer borders through to the next act

The early summer garden encourages us to relax into the display and be fully present as we witness the year's most flamboyant show

Amelanchier × *lamarckii* provides dappled sun for shade-loving perennials beneath, while also drawing the eye upward, making the space feel larger. Climbers such as *Clematis* 'Étoile Violette' trained through roses extend the flowering season and create vertical interest without demanding additional ground space – a technique particularly valuable where every spare spot counts.

When designing early summer borders, if space is limited, I add rhythm by repeating plant forms and shapes, rather than simply duplicating the same plants, so I can pack in more varieties. The vertical spires of salvias with verbascums, the rounded domes of alliums with flowers in various sizes, and the airy froth of *Verbena* × *baileyana* 'Purple Haze' and *Foeniculum vulgare* 'Purpureum' that guides the eye through the garden. This approach maintains coherence while allowing for tremendous diversity in plant selection, perfect for those who, like me, can never resist adding 'just one more' tempting variety.

The early summer garden encourages us to relax into the display and be fully present as we witness the year's most flamboyant show. These perfect weeks when everything seems to flower simultaneously are to be savoured precisely because they won't last forever. By designing with kaleidoscopic tones, we create spaces that capture early summer's essence – its generosity, vitality and intoxicating beauty – while laying the groundwork for the seasons still to come.

Satin Fireworks

Contrasting textures in jewel-toned blooms

This vibrant combination delivers weeks of colour throughout early summer. I love experimenting with different alliums – there's something quite thrilling about discovering varieties beyond the usual suspects. 'Toabago' (formerly 'Spider') at 60cm (2ft) produces firework-like bursts of darker purple stars – a stunning *schubertii* hybrid that's more compact and richly coloured than its parent, creating brilliant vertical drama with its spheres floating above everything else.

The satin-smooth petals of *Papaver somniferum* 'Lauren's Grape' provide jewel-like depth in grape tones, creating perfect contrast with the explosive allium blooms. Fluffy cones of *Trifolium rubens* add cottage garden softness with their delightful pink puffs, while *Papaver rupifragum* 'Flore Pleno's bold orange blooms (just out of shot here, see p.81) add warm tones and bridge the colour spectrum beautifully between the cool violets and deep grape hues. Give them full sun and decent drainage, and watch the pollinators arrive in droves.

Trifolium rubens This underused ornamental clover brings cottage-garden charm with its fluffy pink-purple cones from early to midsummer, the trifoliate leaves adding textural interest before flowering begins. Reaching 50cm (1⅔ ft), it's perfect for the mid-border, and thrives in most soils but appreciates good drainage. Cut back after flowering for a potential second flush. This species attracts bees and butterflies in abundance, making it invaluable for wildlife gardens. HARDINESS: RHS H7

Allium **'Toabago'** A spectacular hybrid between *A. schubertii* and *A. atropurpureum*, creating large blooms in rich purple tones. Each 10cm (4in) flower head produces a starburst of small blooms on stems reaching 60cm (2ft). The sweet fragrance attracts masses of pollinators and it is an excellent cut flower, too. Plant bulbs 10cm (4in) deep in autumn for dramatic displays now.
HARDINESS: RHS H5

Papaver somniferum **'Lauren's Grape'** This stunning poppy produces silk-smooth petals in deep purple-grape tones, creating blooms that seem to glow against the softer textures around them. The flowers appear on sturdy stems and provide rich colour contrast in early summer plantings. Thrives in well-drained soil in full sun.
HARDINESS: RHS H4

Papaver rupifragum **'Flore Pleno'** The Spanish poppy (seen overleaf) produces delicate apricot-orange blooms from late spring through to late summer. Unlike other poppies, it flowers continuously rather than in flushes. The double flowers appear on 40cm (1⅓ft) stems above rosettes of evergreen foliage, and it self-seeds gently, creating natural drifts. This perennial thrives in poor, well-drained soil and full sun.
HARDINESS: RHS H5

> **TIPS FOR SUCCESS**
> - Plant allium bulbs in autumn, positioning taller varieties behind perennials.
> - Deadhead *Papaver ruprifragum* weekly for continuous flowering through summer.
> - Allow some allium seedheads to remain for autumn and winter interest.
> - Water in dry spells but avoid overwatering – these plants prefer good drainage.
> - Divide perennials every 3–4 years to maintain vigour.

Trifolium rubens

Papaver rupifragum 'Flore Pleno'

Opposite *Allium* 'Toabago'

Above *Trifolium rubens* with *Papaver somniferum* 'Lauren's Grape'

Tall story

Purple orbs and graceful giant flowers

This bold palette of rich purples and cream tones brings drama to early summer borders, with vertical elements adding impressive structure. The deep purple globes of *Allium* 'Summer Drummer' float like perfect spheres above everything else, while the towering cream pincushions of *Cephalaria gigantea* rise majestically around them. Rich purple spikes of *Agastache* 'Blackadder' add mid-level colour and incredible fragrance, attracting bees and butterflies.

The split-level borders of my garden allow wonderful opportunities for layering to create even more impact. Plant in full sun with well-drained soil for these plants to thrive, guaranteeing colour from early summer through to late autumn.

Allium **'Summer Drummer'** This spectacular ornamental onion, one of the tallest varieties, produces large, perfectly spherical flowerheads of deep purple-pink that seem to hover on sturdy 1.8m (6ft) tall stems. Blooming in early summer, each globe-shaped flower attracts masses of pollinators and makes excellent cut flowers, indeed I included them in my own wedding bouquet. Plant bulbs 15cm (6in) deep in autumn and allow foliage to die back naturally. **HARDINESS: RHS H5**

Agastache **'Blackadder'** An exceptional perennial with intensely fragrant foliage and rich purple flower spikes that bloom from midsummer into autumn. Reaching 90cm (3ft) tall, it forms neat clumps with aromatic leaves that release their scent when brushed against. Adored by bees and butterflies, it's drought-tolerant once established. **HARDINESS: RHS H4**

Cephalaria gigantea Giant scabious creates light, airy architectural presence with cream-coloured pincushion flowers on towering 2.5m (8ft) stems. The large, deeply divided leaves form impressive clumps, while the flowers appear from early to midsummer, followed by attractive seedheads. This robust perennial self-seeds gently and thrives in most well-drained soils. **HARDINESS: RHS H6**

TIPS FOR SUCCESS

- Plant in full sun with good drainage – most here resent winter wet conditions.
- Add grit to clay soils to improve drainage, particularly important for alliums.
- Remove spent *Agastache* flowers to extend blooming but leave allium and *Cephalaria* seedheads for winter structure.
- Let *Verbena bonariensis* self-seed for natural effect but remove excess seedlings to prevent overcrowding.
- Cut back borderline hardy plants like *Agastache* in spring rather than autumn to protect crowns through winter.

Cephalaria gigantea

Allium 'Summer Drummer'

Above The rich purples and cream tones weave beautifully together

Opposite *Agastache* 'Blackadder'

Summer Fire

Warm oranges and rich purples in prairie harmony

Capturing summer at its most exuberant, this palette of warm oranges and rich purples creates a glowing display from midsummer right through to autumn. The star performers include the distinctive coppery blooms of *Helenium* 'Moerheim Beauty' and the darkest of all sunflowers, *Helianthus annuus* 'Velvet Queen', which brings velvety burgundy drama. Weaving through at different heights, *Allium sphaerocephalon*'s drumstick heads create purple punctuation marks on slender stems that mix beautifully with a variety of plants.

Through the border's progression, the *Allium sphaerocephalon* adds oomph to the emerging spiky blooms of *Echinacea* 'Green Twister', which are calmed by the fine texture of *Bouteloua gracilis*, making the planting delicately prairie-like. All complement one another, drawing in pollinating insects with great success.

Helenium **'Moerheim Beauty'** This classic cultivar produces distinctive daisy-like blooms in rich coppery-red to orange-red tones, with reflexed petals surrounding prominent chocolate-brown centres. The flowers, which measure 6–8cm (2–3½ in) across, are held on wiry 90cm (3ft) stems. This perennial prefers moist but well-drained soil enriched with organic matter. **HARDINESS: RHS H7**

Helianthus annuus **'Velvet Queen'** This elegant annual produces velvety, burgundy-red blooms with dark chocolate centres. The branching habit produces multiple 13cm (5in) flowers on 150–180cm (5–6ft) stems. Sow seed indoors in late spring for earlier blooms (it flowers 75–85 days from sowing). Thriving in any well-drained soil in full sun, space plants 30–45cm (1–1½ft) apart and provide support. **HARDINESS: RHS H4**

Allium sphaerocephalon Drumstick alliums produce egg-shaped flower heads with a fascinating two-tone effect – opening green then turning rich claret-purple from the top down. The bulb grows to 60–90cm (2–3ft) tall on slender stems, which make it a wonderful mixer to weave through grasses and perennials that will help support it. **HARDINESS: RHS H6**

Echinacea **'Green Twister'** This unique coneflower produces spiky, lime-green blooms that mature to show hints of pink and purple. They create striking architectural interest, reaching 60cm (2ft) tall with sturdy stems. Drought-tolerant once established and provides late-season nectar for butterflies. **HARDINESS: RHS H5**

Bouteloua gracilis Known as mosquito grass, this delicate prairie native forms fine tufts of blue-green foliage that cure to attractive golden-buff tones in autumn. Reaching up to 60cm (2ft) tall, it produces distinctive horizontal seedheads that resemble tiny eyebrows dancing in the breeze. This drought-tolerant grass thrives in poor, well-drained soils and full sun, making it perfect for naturalistic plantings. **HARDINESS: RHS H6**

Helianthus annuus 'Velvet Queen' **(top left)**; *Helenium* 'Moerheim Beauty' **(top right)**; rich purples and greens as *Allium sphaerocephalon* takes the foreground **(bottom)**

TIPS FOR SUCCESS

- Sow sunflower seeds outside *in situ* after the last frost, or start indoors four weeks earlier.
- Improve drainage by adding grit to heavier soils for Mediterranean-climate plants such as the alliums and echinacea.
- Deadhead spent *Helenium* flowers weekly for extended flowering but leave echinacea seedheads for winter structure and bird food.
- Provide discrete support for sunflowers and tall *Heleniums* in exposed positions to prevent wind damage to stems.
- Allow *Bouteloua gracilis* to remain standing through winter for structure, cutting back in late winter before new growth begins.

Shade Sanctuary

Ethereal blooms and textured foliage for cool spots

Cream and white plants add light to shady areas, transforming them into serene sanctuaries, proving that subtle colour can be just as impactful as bold displays. Star-like white blooms create a luminous framework: *Astrantia major* subsp. *involucrata* 'Shaggy' floats its distinctive pincushions above *Alchemilla mollis*'s acid-yellow froth, while pure white *Centranthus ruber* 'Albus' catches the eye in darker corners. Supporting the scene, elsewhere in the planting gentle purple spires of *Digitalis purpurea* add vertical interest.

With varied heights to create wonderful depth, this soft palette reflects precious light and creates a cooling effect that's a joy to sit among on a hot day. The combination is perfect for bringing gentle colour to shady borders or beneath deciduous trees.

Alchemilla mollis This cottage garden stalwart produces clouds of acid-yellow flowers above scalloped leaves that catch water droplets like jewels. Growing to 45cm (1½ft), it self-seeds gently, creating lovely ground cover, and the flowers last for weeks when cut. *Alchemilla* tolerates most soils and aspects. Cut back after flowering for fresh new foliage. **HARDINESS: RHS H7**

Astrantia major **subsp.** ***involucrata*** **'Shaggy'** This perennial produces distinctive white flowers with elongated, green-tipped bracts that create an undone, soft, shaggy appearance in a border, which is hugely welcome. It reaches up to 75cm (2½ft) and flowers for months, if deadheaded, the blooms also lasting well in a vase. It thrives in moist, humus-rich soil. Divide every few years. **HARDINESS: RHS H7**

Centranthus ruber **'Albus'** The white form of red valerian brings brightness to difficult shady spots. Fragrant flowers that attract masses of pollinators appear from late spring and throughout summer on 60cm (2ft) stems. Incredibly drought-tolerant once established, this perennial thrives in poor, alkaline soil. It also self-seeds readily – deadhead to control spread. **HARDINESS: RHS H5**

TIPS FOR SUCCESS

- Keep the soil consistently moist during active growth periods from spring to summer.
- Deadhead astrantias and the *Centranthus* to extend flowering.
- Cut back *Alchemilla* after flowering to encourage fresh new foliage.
- Allow some plants to self-seed to create a natural effect.

Astrantia major subsp. *involucrata* 'Shaggy' **(top left)**; *Centranthus ruber* 'Albus' **(top right)**; *Alchemilla mollis* **(bottom)**

Heritage Heights

Old fashioned sweet peas for summer-long fragrance

It wouldn't be summer here without garden arches of sweet peas trained into fragrant summer tapestries. I favour a nostalgic collection of heritage varieties for their exceptional perfume – the very quality so often lost in modern breeding – which drifts through warm evenings, while the blooms deliver fistfuls of posies for months, if plants are kept fed and watered. The richly scented 'Matucana' mingles with velvety 'Black Knight' and the unusual orange 'Henry Eckford', while 'Lord Nelson's true navy complements the deepest maroon. The historic 'Cupani', with its celebrated 1699 fragrance (see right), adds proper sweet pea authenticity. These smaller Grandiflora types might lack the size of modern Spencers, but their intense colours and heavenly scent explain why they've been treasured for generations. I plant fennel's acid-yellow umbels close by for added fragrance and to provide the perfect foil for all those jewel tones. Sometimes the originals really are the best.

Lathyrus odoratus **'Matucana'** The queen of scented sweet peas in my opinion, producing bi-coloured blooms of deep purple and maroon with exceptional fragrance. More vigorous than its ancestor 'Cupani' (although I grow both), this heritage variety flowers prolifically on 1.8m (6ft) stems. Reportedly the strongest scented sweet pea in the world, it holds an RHS Award of Garden Merit. HARDINESS: RHS H3

Lathyrus odoratus **'Henry Eckford'** A favourite of mine, this unusual orange variety proving that warm-toned sweet peas can smell divine. Named after the Scottish breeder who revolutionised sweet pea breeding, it combines sunset shades with huge fragrance. Reaching 1.5m (5ft), it has slightly smaller blooms than modern varieties but makes up for it in perfume. HARDINESS: RHS H3

Lathyrus odoratus **'Black Knight'** Deep maroon blooms that appear almost black at dusk create dramatic impact on this heritage variety, introduced by Henry Eckford in 1898. It brings scent and dramatic colour, too, perfect for adding mystery to mixed displays. HARDINESS: RHS H3

Lathyrus odoratus **'Lord Nelson'** True navy-blue flowers are rare in the garden, making this variety indispensable for sweet pea connoisseurs. Another Eckford triumph, this early 1900s introduction combines deep colour with a strong scent. HARDINESS: RHS H3

Lathyrus odoratus **'Cupani'** The original sweet pea, discovered in Sicily in 1699 by a monk, Franciscus Cupani, who then introduced it to Britain. It produces smaller, daintier flowers than 'Matucana', with only two per stem, but with incredible historical significance and intense fragrance. The bi-coloured purple and maroon blooms appear on 1.5m (5ft) stems. HARDINESS: RHS H3

TIPS FOR SUCCESS

- Sow seeds indoors in midwinter in root trainers (tall seed modules).
- Move seedlings to cold frames once four pairs of leaves appear.
- Plant out in spring, 15cm (6in) apart next to tall supports.
- Feed weekly once flowering starts with high-potassium fertiliser.
- Pick flowers regularly – the more you cut, the more they bloom.
- Save seed from the best plants for next year's display.

Fire in the Shadows

Hot colours for a cool, shady border

Who says borders with limited sunlight have to be subtle? This fearless combination proves that bold colour can thrive in challenging aspects, bringing warmth and drama to traditionally cool spaces.

The star performer is *Hemerocallis* 'Stafford', whose rich burgundy-red trumpets glow like embers in the shade. These edible flowers (did you know you can eat the blooms – ideal for perking up a salad?) partner well with the architectural foliage of *Rodgersia podophylla* 'Braunlaub', whose bronze-tinted leaves create the perfect backdrop. *Rosa* NIGHT OWL frames the entire composition with its dusky purple blooms, while the acid-green fronds of the shuttlecock fern (*Matteuccia struthiopteris*) add height and fresh leafy contrast. Come late summer, *Crocosmia* 'Lucifer' takes over the colour baton with its flame-red torches arching over the *Hemerocallis* clumps.

The secret to success? Plant in moisture-retentive, humus-rich soil – these shade-tolerant performers need consistent moisture to support their bold displays.

Hemerocallis 'Stafford' Arguably the finest red daylily, producing rich burgundy-red flowers with golden throats on stems 75cm (2½ft) tall from early to midsummer. Each bloom lasts just one day but plants produce dozens of buds. Beware of hemerocallis gall midge in some areas. This perennial thrives in sun or partial shade. **HARDINESS: RHS H6**

Rodgersia podophylla 'Braunlaub' This architectural perennial produces huge palmate leaves with bronze tints, particularly pronounced in spring and autumn, with creamy flower plumes appearing in midsummer on 1.2m (4ft) stems. Perfect for adding structure to shady borders, simply edit out excess leaves where you don't want them. It requires consistently moist soil and shelter from strong winds. **HARDINESS: RHS H7**

Rosa NIGHT OWL This is a superb climber, with fragrant, deep purple blooms that repeat throughout summer. Reaching 3m (10ft) in height, it's ideal for training on walls or fences. The dusky flowers provide a sophisticated contrast to the bright daylily, while picking up on the *Rodgersia* foliage tones. It has good disease-resistance for a rose. Deadhead regularly for continuous blooming. **HARDINESS: RHS H6**

Matteuccia struthiopteris A deciduous fern with magnificent fresh green fronds arranged in perfect shuttlecock formation that reach 90–120cm (3–4ft). The sterile fronds emerge in spring and are followed by distinctive brown fertile fronds in late summer. It spreads by underground runners – perfect for naturalising in damp shade. Excellent for adding vertical structure. Cut back dead fronds in late winter. **HARDINESS: RHS H7**

TIPS FOR SUCCESS

- Enrich the soil annually with organic matter to help it retain moisture.
- Water thoroughly during dry spells – these plants need consistent moisture.
- Divide *Hemerocallis* every 3–4 years to maintain vigour.
- Train rose carefully on horizontal wires or supports to maximise flowering (see p.103).
- Control spread of *Matteuccia* and *Rodgersia* by removing unwanted runners.

Rosa NIGHT OWL **(top left)**; *Hemerocallis* 'Stafford' **(top right)**; *Rodgersia podophylla* 'Braunlaub' and *Matteuccia struthiopteris* **(bottom)**

Purple Haze

Sophisticated tones in gentle light

This sophisticated combination delivers months of colour in a border that doesn't receive much light. The rich burgundy stars of *Astrantia* 'Burgundy Manor' create depth alongside distinctive maroon-burgundy drumstick heads with their tufted tops on arching stems. In the foreground, the architectural seedhead of *Allium* 'Toabago' adds structural interest, while the emerging foliage of *Anemone* 'Pamina' promises autumn colour to come. A sprinkling of *Sesleria autumnalis* provides delicate textural interest at ground level.

This group thrives in dappled sunshine and partial shade, making it perfect for those challenging spots where many plants struggle. The combination provides interest from early summer right through the growing season, with the *Astrantia* flowering continuously and the allium's architectural seedheads persisting long after the blooms fade. All attract pollinators during their flowering periods, bringing life to quieter corners of the garden.

***Allium* 'Forelock'** This distinctive ornamental onion produces maroon-burgundy, egg-shaped heads on bending stems. Reaching 60cm (2ft) tall (taller if it's especially happy!), the globed flowerheads appear in early summer, followed by attractive seedheads that provide structure through autumn. The unusual, curved stems create a softer, more naturalistic effect than rigid upright alliums. Thrives in well-drained soil. **HARDINESS: RHS H5**

***Astrantia* 'Burgundy Manor'** This superior selection produces masses of rich burgundy-red pincushion flowers on stems reaching 70–90cm (2⅓–3ft). The star-shaped blooms rise above mounds of palmate foliage and flower from early summer, with a main flush and possible rebloom after cutting back. Thrives in partial shade and moisture-retentive, humus-rich soils but tolerates most conditions with adequate mulching. Exceptional as a cut flower with good vase life. **HARDINESS: RHS H7**

Sesleria autumnalis Autumn moor grass forms neat, compact tufts of fine blue-green foliage that provide excellent textural contrast at ground level. This hardy perennial grass reaches 60cm (2ft) tall and produces tall, upright panicles of creamy-white flowers in late summer and autumn. Neat evergreen, clumping foliage creates attractive year-round structure, and it tolerates poor soils and partial shade, making it perfect for challenging spots. **HARDINESS: RHS H7**

TIPS FOR SUCCESS

- Position allium bulbs in autumn to emerge through perennial clumps, creating natural-looking drifts in the border.
- Water *Astrantia* during dry spellsto keep foliage fresh but ensure good drainage to prevent winter waterlogging.
- Deadhead *Astrantia* occasionally for tidiness, though it's not essential.
- Allow *Sesleria* to self-seed naturally but thin excess seedlings to prevent overcrowding of other plants.
- Divide *Astrantia* clumps every 3 years in spring to maintain vigour and prevent overcrowding in the border.

WHAT TO DO
EARLY SUMMER

Early summer sees the garden at its most exuberant. Those bold colour combinations we've been nurturing finally take centre stage – deep purples mingling with hot oranges, cool blues offsetting warm yellows. While it's tempting to simply admire the display during these weeks of peak colour, thoughtful maintenance can make all the difference, when borders need our attention to look their best now and in the months ahead. It's satisfying work – each task directly enhancing the garden's performance and your enjoyment of it.

Planting Out Dahlias

If you've been growing dahlia tubers in pots and haven't yet planted them out, early summer provides the perfect window. The soil is properly warmed and all frost risks have passed, allowing these flamboyant beauties to establish quickly.

Dahlias thrive equally well in borders or containers in sunny spots. For pots, choose containers at least 40cm (1⅓ft) deep for larger varieties – I plant almost all of mine this way for maximum flexibility in my displays through the year. Use peat-free multipurpose compost mixed with slow-release fertiliser, planting the tubers with their growing points just below the surface.

In borders, choose positions in full sun where their bright colours will really sing. They need rich soil, so work in plenty of compost before planting. Space according to eventual size – dinner-plate varieties need 90cm (3ft) between plants, while smaller bedding types manage with 45cm (1½ft).

Insert stakes now to avoid damaging tubers, stems and flowers later. Whether in pots or the ground, dahlias pair brilliantly with late summer performers – try deep burgundy varieties alongside orange crocosmias, or pink forms with purple salvias. The Bishop varieties with dark foliage look particularly striking threading through border plantings to give rhythm and dynamism.

Strategic Deadheading

Deadheading in early summer goes beyond simply tidying – it's about extending colour displays and managing plant energy. Different flowering plants need different approaches to keep them performing at their best.

Roses require precision cuts to maintain their colour contribution. Cut stems back at an angle, just above the first leaf stem with five leaflets, immediately below the faded flower. For floribundas that produce clusters of blooms, remove entire trusses once most of the flowers have faded. Shrub roses benefit from lighter treatment, preserving their natural form.

Sweet peas demand daily picking – the more blooms you harvest, the longer they'll produce those wonderful pastels or rich burgundies. Similarly, dahlias and cosmos respond brilliantly to regular deadheading, keeping colour flowing well into autumn.

Perennials need careful consideration; many plants can be encouraged to give a second flush with a good cut back now. However, preserve some for their architectural seed heads over winter – metallic eryngiums and structural echinaceas add textural interest, while feeding birds later in the year.

Sourcing Autumn-Flowering Bulbs

While everyone's focused on summer's display, forward-thinking gardeners are buying autumn-flowering bulbs. These often-overlooked gems provide unexpected colour when most gardens begin to wind down.

Nerines top my list – their shocking pink or white blooms appear on naked stems, creating dramatic statements in early autumn. Plant them in hot, dry spots against sunlight-facing walls where they'll bake in summer heat. Also consider colchicums, which offer large crocus-like flowers in shades of pink and purple, and are perfect for naturalising under shrubs.

Autumn-flowering crocus species such as *Crocus speciosus* and *C. sativus* (the saffron crocus) create carpets of blue or purple, and establish well in grass and gravel gardens. *Cyclamen hederifolium* starts flowering in early autumn, too, its marbled leaves providing winter interest long after the flowers fade.

Order these speciality bulbs now while nurseries have good stocks. They're often sold out by late summer when most gardeners remember them. Plant nerines immediately but hold off planting other autumn bulbs until late summer for best results.

Managing Self-Seeders

While self-seeders add spontaneity to planting schemes, they need managing to prevent total chaos.

Alchemilla mollis drops thousands of seeds – delightful in moderation but overwhelming if left unchecked. Cut back flower heads before seeds ripen if you've enough plants – the same applies to bronze fennel (*Foeniculum vulgare* 'Purpureum'), *Verbena bonariensis* and evening primrose (*Oenothera biennis*). I leave some to self-sow but remove others strategically, maintaining colour balance, while allowing natural effects.

Welsh poppies and forget-me-nots can carpet borders beautifully but may also smother your favourite plants if you don't watch their step. Thin ruthlessly, keeping only those in prime positions. Your compost heap will appreciate the green material, and you'll maintain the intended colour harmony you were after, rather than descending into botanical mayhem.

Summer Pruning for Shape and Vigour

Unlike spring's structural pruning, summer pruning shapes plants and controls vigour, while maintaining season-long colour.

Wisteria needs summer pruning to encourage flower bud formation. Cut back whippy side shoots to five or six leaves from the main framework. This concentrates energy into developing next year's purple or white cascades, rather than excessive leafy growth.

Early-flowering shrubs like mock orange (*Philadelphus*) benefit from post-bloom pruning. Remove a third of the old stems at ground level, encouraging fresh growth.

Successional Planting for Continuous Colour

As spring bulbs fade and early perennials finish, gaps can appear in our carefully planned schemes. Early summer's warmth provides perfect conditions for filling these spaces. When my containers are planted up, I keep back-up pots of annuals, using them to fill bare patches – zinnias in hot pinks and oranges, rudbeckias with mahogany daisies, or cosmos in every shade of pink. These instant solutions maintain colour flow while later perennials develop.

Also consider direct sowing quick-maturing annuals. Nasturtiums scramble through established plantings, their orange and yellow flowers adding warmth. Night-scented stocks (*Matthiola longipetala* subsp. *bicornis*) provide evening fragrance alongside daytime colour. Annual poppies self-sow readily once established, creating natural drifts of sunset shades – *Papaver somniferum* 'Lauren's Grape' is an absolute favourite of mine to scatter at whim.

Supporting Heavy Flowers

Early summer's lush growth produces heavy blooms that need discrete support before they flop.

Peonies' dinner-plate-sized blooms collapse dramatically after rain. Install grow-through supports early or use linking stakes around clumps. The metalwork disappears among foliage while preventing those gorgeous blooms from face-planting.

Vertical perennials need thoughtful staking. Sanguisorbas wave burgundy bottlebrushes that keel over without support. Verbascums send up tall spires of yellow or purple that require individual canes. Veronicastrums, with their elegant spikes, benefit from discrete stakes positioned early in summer.

MY ESSENTIAL DOS AND DON'TS

+ Deadhead roses carefully to maintain their colour contribution.
+ Pick sweet peas daily to extend their flowering season.
+ Plant dahlia tubers in pots or borders with support stakes.
+ Thin self-seeders to prevent them overwhelming choice plants.
+ Summer-prune wisteria to encourage next year's flowers.
+ Fill gaps with quick-growing annuals for continuous colour.
+ Remove one-third of old wood from early flowering shrubs.
+ Cut back *Alchemilla mollis* before it seeds everywhere.
+ Feed container displays weekly with high-potassium fertiliser.

− Let bronze fennel self-seed unchecked through borders (unless you love it!).
− Forget to stake tall perennials like sanguisorbas and veronicastrums before they develop top-heavy blooms.
− Miss the chance to order unusual autumn-flowering bulbs, like nerines and colchicums.
− Allow vigorous climbers to smother their neighbours.

The Hampton Hack

Rejuvenate your early summer bloomers with this simple pruning technique

Named after the RHS Hampton Court Palace Garden Festival in early summer, the Hampton Hack is essentially cutting plants back after they've flowered. This technique encourages fresh foliage and often a second flush of flowers on plants that have already performed. It's perfect for rejuvenating tired early-summer perennials and getting more blooms for very little effort.

1 Identify suitable plants
Look for early-flowering perennials that have just finished blooming and are starting to look a bit tired and straggly. There are plenty of plants to cut back now, including hardy geraniums (*Geranium sylvaticum*, *G. endressii*, *G. phaeum*), *Alchemilla mollis*, *Brunnera*, *Nepeta* and early salvias like 'Mainacht'. These plants all naturally regrow from their bases.

2 Be bold with your tools
Blunt tools create messy cuts that invite problems, so think more 'courageous cut' than 'blunt hack'! I carry my diamond sharpener in my pocket so it's close to hand when I need it. Shears are quicker for mass cutting, while secateurs offer extra control, but this is more about decisive action than delicate surgery. You're essentially giving tired plants a fresh start. Clean tools also help to prevent disease.

3 Cut right to the base
Remove all growth to just above ground level – typically about 10cm (4in) or less. With hardy geraniums and alchemilla, if you spot fresh basal foliage emerging, cut just above these new leaves. The hormones in top growth normally suppress basal shoots from developing, and removing such top growth triggers vigorous regrowth.

4 Clear everything away if plants self-seed readily
Chopping and dropping plant trimmings back on to the border is, on the whole, a very good idea, but with prolific self-seeders such as *Alchemilla mollis*, add clippings to your compost bin instead to prevent their unwanted spread.

5 Feed and water well
After such dramatic treatment, plants need encouragement. Apply a balanced fertiliser and water thoroughly. Add a 5cm (2in) layer of well-rotted compost as mulch, keeping it clear of plant crowns. In drought conditions, delay the hack until after rainfall – moisture is crucial for successful regrowth.

6 Watch the transformation
Stand back and you'll see your border has transformed from tired and messy to clean and ready for round two. Fresh growth appears within days to weeks, depending on the conditions. Many plants, particularly hardy geraniums like ROZANNE, produce a second flush of flowers lasting well into autumn. The new growth is also typically more compact and healthier than the original. Your reward? Rejuvenated borders with fresh foliage and extended flowering when other gardens are flagging.

Controlling Wayward Climbers
The pocket twine solution to the best vertical displays

My summer pockets bulge with pre-cut twine lengths – a practical habit that's saved countless climbing displays. Clematis, honeysuckle and jasmine inevitably choose the worst moments to launch themselves in the wrong directions, but a quick intervention can create stunning vertical tapestries if you catch them before they become hopelessly tangled.

1 Always be prepared
Pre-cut natural garden twine into 30cm (1ft) lengths during quiet moments, and keep your pockets full of them whenever you're outside. Ready ties mean immediate action rather than good intentions.

2 Understand growth habits
Before tying anything, observe natural growth patterns. Clematis climbs by wrapping leaf stems around supports to grip, honeysuckle uses twining stems to climb, sweet peas spiral clockwise, and jasmine throws out long whips that need immediate guidance.

3 Perfect the figure-of-eight
Never strangle stems with direct ties. Create a figure-of-eight with your twine (see p.64), which allows natural movement and growth. Leave room for stems to thicken, and use two strands of twine for weighty stems.

4 Think horizontal for flowers
For flower-covered walls train growth horizontally wherever possible. Vertical stems race skyward, flowering only at the tips. Gently bend young shoots sideways at 45-degree angles or more, securing every 30cm (1ft). This slows sap flow, encouraging flowering buds along the entire stem length.

5 Combine climbers creatively
Weave different varieties together for season-long interest. Thread late-flowering clematis through early roses – 'Etoile Violette' partnered with 'Madame Alfred Carrière' creates complementary colour for months. Plant clematis on the shady side of host plants for best results. Guide annual morning glories (*Ipomoea tricolor*) through permanent frameworks, such as hazel wigwams, with other flowers or peas or beans, to give these edibles extra flower oomph. These combinations maximise impact without requiring extra space.

6 Consider propagation by layering
Early summer is perfect for layering climbers – creating new plants while stems are still attached to the parent. Clematis, honeysuckle and jasmine all respond well to this technique. Bend flexible shoots to ground level and pin down with wire or weight with a stone. Cover with soil, leaving the tip exposed. Roots form over summer so that by autumn or the following spring, you can sever the stem attaching the baby to the parent to create free plants ready to transplant. It's an easy way to multiply your favourite climbers *in situ* without the bother of taking cuttings.

Late Summer

The garden's soundtrack shifts noticeably at this time of year – children's laughter carries across lawns still warm from the day's sunshine, wood pigeons coo lazily from treetops, and the soft rustle of ornamental grasses becomes more pronounced as their seed heads mature and catch the evening breeze.

Borders achieve a lushness that reflects the season's accumulated warmth, while the palette deepens toward richer tones that seem to absorb the honeyed sunshine. Light becomes more golden than the clear brightness of early summer, casting longer shadows across gardens as they reach a magnificent maturity. There's a sense of fullness, of completion, as if the garden is at ease with itself, as if this height and fullness of bloom have been there forever, rather than something we've coaxed along all year.

I've always found a special kind of wonder in these weeks, when gardens relax in a way that feels both voluptuous and slightly untamed. The urgency of spring planting and early summer maintenance gives way to a more steady and relaxed relationship with the garden. Now we can sit back and appreciate the results of earlier efforts, watching as butterflies drift between echinaceas and seed heads begin to form, promising food for the birds through winter and self-sown surprises.

This seasonal pivot brings more than just visual changes. The scents transform, too – if late spring is the fragrance of freshly cut grass, then barbecues are very definitely the aroma of late summer! But it's the plant scents I prefer – where the sweet perfume of early summer gives way to fragrances that reflect the richness of the garden's colours. At this time of year, we experience more aromatic notes: the aniseed scent of fennel, the spicy fragrance of *Nicotiana*, and the heady vanilla perfume of *Trachelospermum*. These sensory

Sweet pea-scented pathways through late summer's abundance – this is when the garden feels both voluptuous and slightly wild, exactly as it should

shifts create a garden experience that feels distinctly different from earlier months – more mellow, perhaps, but no less engaging.

When designing for late summer colour, I embrace a palette dominated by hot, saturated hues that stand up to the stronger light. I encourage the garden's last hurrah with copper oranges, regal purples and vivid crimsons which take centre stage now, creating glowing intensity as the sun begins its earlier descent. This is the moment for bold combinations that might have seemed excessive earlier but now feel perfectly in tune with the season.

For reliable flower-power in these high-summer weeks, I rely on daisy-shaped blooms that bring structural clarity to billowing borders. *Rudbeckia fulgida* var. *sullivantii* 'Goldsturm', with its golden-yellow flowers and dark centres, creates swathes of sunshine even on cloudy days, while aromatic *Monarda* 'Scorpion' adds height and architectural presence as its whorls of shaggy red-purple flowers unfurl above deep purple bracts. These combine beautifully with the violet-blue flowers of *Salvia* 'Amistad', whose upright, branching stems add strong vertical accents and height, providing a striking contrast to the looser forms of surrounding perennials. And then, of course, there are the dahlias; more on those later.

The transparent qualities of ornamental grasses become particularly valuable now, their feathery flower heads catching low evening light and creating a diaphanous layer through which other plants can be glimpsed. *Calamagrostis brachytricha* arches over borders, its fluffy, purple-tinged, plume-like sprays of flowers swaying elegantly above lower-growing perennials. *Panicum virgatum* 'Shenandoah' brings rich burgundy tones to the late summer palette, its leaves turning wine-red as the season progresses, while the arching flower heads create a fountain-like effect. I position these grasses where they'll be backlit by evening

When designing for late summer colour, I embrace a palette dominated by hot, saturated hues that stand up to the stronger light

The irresistible *Dahlia* 'Waltzing Mathilda' – proving that late summer's hot palette needs both single blooms for busy bees and a few indulgent, flouncy doubles for sheer joy

sun, transforming them into glowing sentinels that seem to capture the essence of the season.

Gardens with challenging conditions need thoughtful plant selection as the summer advances. For hot, sunny positions, I turn to Mediterranean plants that thrive here – *Salvia* 'Blue Spire' (formerly *Perovskia*) creates clouds of lavender-blue flowers on silvery stems, while white gaura (*Oenothera lindheimeri* 'Whirling Butterflies') adds movement, with its dancing flowers that seem to float above neighbouring plants. These drought-tolerant performers deliver weeks of reliable colour while requiring little moisture – an increasingly important consideration as summers become hotter and drier.

Shadier sites needn't lack late summer colour interest. I rely on the rich violet-blue flowers of *Aconitum carmichaelii* (Arendsii Group) 'Arendsii', whose tall spires bring valuable late colour to woodland edges. The white wands of *Actaea simplex* (Atropurpurea Group) 'Brunette' (formerly *Cimicifuga*) rising above bronze-purple foliage add both architectural presence and delicious fragrance to areas that might otherwise lack interest as summer progresses. These shade-lovers demonstrate that every part of the garden can contribute to the seasonal display, regardless of conditions.

Texture plays an increasingly important role in the late summer garden. With seed heads beginning to form even as new flowers continue to open, I deliberately incorporate plants with distinctive architectural qualities that will extend interest into autumn – the spherical seed heads of *Echinops*, the starry calyces of Chinese lanterns (*Physalis alkekengi*), the structural umbels of *Angelica gigas*

Geraniums – summer's essential stalwarts threading through borders, linking everything together with their gentle sprawl and weeks of dependable colour

Reliable annuals such as *Salvia viridis* 'Oxford Blue' keep the nectar flowing when summer starts to fade **(left)**; dahlias and sunflowers are still blazing and ornamental grasses come into their own, everything performing together before autumn takes over **(right)**

all provide valuable form as the season advances. Remember that shades of buff, camel and brown are colours, too. These elements will continue to earn their keep long after their flowers have faded, catching frost and snow to create winter interest.

The late summer garden encourages us to notice details that might be overlooked in the more obvious beauty of earlier seasons. It rewards close observation – the perfect symmetry of a sunflower's seed pattern, the delicate colour blend on a dahlia petal, the tracery of veins on translucent grass flowers. These close encounters reveal a garden of intricate details that the exuberance of early summer might have overshadowed.

I absolutely adore late summer's deeper, richer colours and the architectural character that seed heads bring to borders. It's a special time to appreciate both current beauty and future potential hiding in those developing seed pods. That's the thing about gardens – they're always holding the past, present and future all at once, if you just take the time to notice.

Drifting into Late Summer

Warm colours for summer's end

This late summer combination has a wafting, meadow-like quality that keeps things interesting when other borders are beginning to look tired. The acid-yellow umbels of dill (*Anethum graveolens*) create 60–80cm (2–2⅔ft) structure, while *Pennisetum orientale* 'Flamingo' adds kinetic interest with rose-pink inflorescences. The colour harmony works particularly well, with *Trifolium rubens* providing vertical purple accents that echo the *Pennisetum*'s tones, creating visual continuity. Meanwhile, warm orange ray florets of *Ratibida columnifera* f. *pulcherrima* and papery tangerine *Papaver rupifragum* form a bridge between them. It's a scheme that really comes into its own from midsummer onwards, offering plenty for visiting pollinators, too. This naturalistic style also suits my approach perfectly – less fiddling about and more time to enjoy the results with a cuppa.

TIPS FOR SUCCESS

- Arrange in relaxed drifts, letting plants mingle at the edges for a natural look.
- Sow dill (*Anethum graveolens*) directly where it's to flower; thin seedlings to about 20–25cm (8–10in) apart.
- Keep deadheading poppies and Mexican hats (*Ratibida*) to extend flowering well into autumn.
- Cut clover (*Trifolium*) back hard after its first flowering for a good late summer encore.
- Leave seed heads standing over winter – they look lovely with frost and birds appreciate them.
- Let some plants self-seed to maintain that meadow feel and fill any bare patches.

***Anethum graveolens* 'Mariska'** This florist's dill has proved much sturdier than regular dill in my mixed borders, and it flowers earlier, too. The yellow umbels last well and don't flop about like some varieties. I combine sowing clumps into pots then planting out, and direct sowing where I want it to flower, as it doesn't always transplant well. If you have the time, successional sowing every fortnight keeps the display going nicely. The leaves and flowers are edible, too. **HARDINESS: RHS H4**

***Pennisetum orientale* 'Flamingo'** Pink plumes are slow to start, but appear just when you need them in late summer. At around 75cm (2½ft) tall, they catch the light beautifully without overwhelming smaller plants. Remember to wait until you see new growth in spring before cutting back this deciduous form. Spring planting works best to get this grass established. **HARDINESS: RHS H3**

Trifolium rubens This ornamental clover has become a reliable favourite. The red cylindrical flowers appear in early summer, but a good chop after flowering usually produces a second flush for late summer. Being a clover, it helps improve the soil, too. Bees absolutely love it, and it copes well with dry spells once settled in. **HARDINESS: RHS H7**

Ratibida columnifera* f. *pulcherrima Mexican hat always makes me smile, with its drooping yellow petals and prominent brown centres. It flowers continuously from early summer through to autumn if you keep deadheading. Thriving in poor soil where fussier plants struggle, it self-seeds just enough to fill gaps without taking over. The seed heads look good in winter, too. **HARDINESS: RHS H6**

Papaver rupifragum This Spanish poppy has surprised me with its staying power. The orange flowers keep coming from early summer right through to the last frost, if deadheaded regularly. It's short-lived (about 2–3 years) but self-sows reliably. Particularly happy in well-drained spots, it doesn't mind a bit of drought. **HARDINESS: RHS H5**

Ratibida columnifera f. *pulcherrima*

Trifolium rubens with *Geum* 'Totally Tangerine' behind

Opposite *Anethum graveolens* 'Mariska'   **Above** *Pennisetum orientale* 'Flamingo'

Gentle Giants

Soft textures deliver a quiet beauty

Come late summer, my garden develops a lovely soft focus – not blurred exactly, but gentler somehow. This combination captures that mood perfectly. I've woven together the aster *Symphyotrichum* 'Vasterival' and Korean feather reed grass (*Calamagrostis brachytricha*) to create something that feels both spontaneous and sophisticated. The secret? It's all about the light. Plant these where late afternoon sun can work through the feathery grass plumes and dance across those tiny aster flowers, and you'll understand why I'm still pottering about with a gin and tonic at dusk. This duo thrives in average garden soil with decent drainage and will keep performing from midsummer right through to the first frosts. The lavender-buff palette creates a dream quality that makes everything else surrounding it in the border look better too.

***Symphyotrichum* 'Vasterival'** Flowering from late summer onwards, clouds of lilac-pink daisies with yellow centres emerge from deep pink buds, creating a gorgeous colour progression. At 1.2m (4ft) tall, with dark, multi-branched stems, it's architectural yet see-through – perfect for mid-border where its open habit lets you glimpse the plants growing behind it.
HARDINESS: RHS H7

Calamagrostis brachytricha Korean feather reed grass is my go-to for adding movement without drama. Its pink-tinged plumes emerge in late summer, catching every breeze and glowing when backlit. Reaching 90–120cm (3–4ft), it's architectural without being overpowering.
HARDINESS: RHS H6

> **TIPS FOR SUCCESS**
> - Give plants room to breathe – asters need 50cm (1⅔ft) between them; allow the grass 90cm (3ft) clearance.
> - Position ornamental grasses where afternoon sun can backlight the flowers and seed heads.

Calamagrostis brachytricha **(right)**; *Symphyotrichum* 'Vasterival' **(opposite)**

Late Summer

Vertical Voltage

Spikes and sprays that steal the show

There's something deeply satisfying about this combination that makes me smile every time I pass it. I've woven together a constellation of spikes – those magnificent verbascum candelabras with their violet-eyed golden blooms, elegant verbenas in every shade of purple, and aromatic agastache – while those reliable crocosmia wands thread through like warm honey.

The verbascum really steals the show here, those branching flower towers absolutely luminous against all the purple tones. It's theatrical without being overwhelming, elegant yet relaxed. I adore the play between warm yellows and cool purples and blues – it creates a rhythm that draws the eye upward and keeps it dancing.

Plant this little lot in full sun with decent drainage, and you'll have non-stop colour through to the first proper frosts. It's exactly the sort of generous display that makes you chuckle so loudly your neighbours peer over the fence and ask what on earth you've been up to!

Verbascum chaixii **'Sixteen Candles'** The star of this show, and rightly so. Those golden flower spikes with violet filaments rise like illuminated candelabras to 90cm (3ft), branching beautifully as they mature. Starts flowering in late spring and keeps going all summer if you deadhead regularly – just cut the spent spikes right back and more will follow. Watch out for the spectacular yellow and black striped mullein moth caterpillars – they can make a real mess of the leaves but are easily picked off. Self-seeds readily, so you'll always have backup plants coming along.
HARDINESS: RHS H5

Crocosmia × crocosmiiflora **'George Davison'** This Edwardian classic still holds its own against flashier modern cultivars. Its golden yellow flowers, opening from orange buds, bloom earlier than most montbretias on 90cm (3ft) stems, starting midsummer and carrying on for weeks. It spreads steadily – just lift, divide and share the extras. The arching sprays add graceful movement among all those upright spikes. **HARDINESS: RHS H5**

Verbena bonariensis The ultimate see-through plant, those purple clusters seem to float on wiry 1.2–1.5m (4–5ft) stems. Self-seeds with enthusiasm (which I rather like), creating happy accidents throughout the border. Butterflies queue up for it, and those delicate stems bend rather than break in wind. **HARDINESS: RHS H4**

Verbena hastata **f.** *rosea* The pink form of blue vervain brings softer tones to the mix with those slender 60–120cm (2–4ft) spikes blooming from bottom to top. Native to North American prairies, it's tough as old boots and brilliant for attracting specialist bees. The vertical habit adds structural backbone while the pink flowers bridge between purples and oranges beautifully.
HARDINESS: RHS H5

$\rightarrow$

> **TIPS FOR SUCCESS**
> - Plant in full sun with well-drained soil – most hate winter wet.
> - Allow *Verbena bonariensis* to self-seed for naturalistic drifts.
> - Divide crocosmia clumps every 3–4 years when congested.
> - Cut agastache back by half in spring to prevent woody growth.
> - Plant in odd-numbered groups for the most natural effect.

Crocosmia × *crocosmiiflora* 'George Davison'

Verbena × baileyana 'Purple Haze' A hybrid combining the long flowering season and dark leaves of *Verbena officinalis* 'Bampton' with the showier flower heads of *Verbena hastata rosea*. Purple-pink flowers up to 1m (3⅓ft) from early summer to early autumn, more compact than *V. bonariensis* but equally loved by butterflies and bees. HARDINESS: RHS H4

Agastache 'Blackadder' Those deep purple-blue flower spikes on 60–90cm (2–3ft) stems smell divine when brushed against – like liquorice and mint combined. Flowers from midsummer through to autumn, with bees working it constantly. The narrow, aromatic leaves create excellent textural contrast. Can be short-lived but usually self-seeds if it's happy. HARDINESS: RHS H4

Above *Agastache* 'Blackadder'
Opposite *Verbena* × *baileyana* 'Purple Haze'

Verbascum chaixii 'Sixteen Candles'

Late Summer

Sun Meets Shade

Bridging bright and shady spots with late summer colour

Dealing with that tricky transition where sun meets shade is always a challenge. Here, I've used the flaming torches of *Crocosmia* 'Lucifer' reaching for the light at the brighter end, while the shuttlecock-shaped *Matteuccia struthiopteris* thrives in the shadier depths. Between them, *Veronicastrum virginicum* 'Fascination' creates elegant purple candelabras that bridge both worlds. The silvery plumes of *Miscanthus sinensis* add essential movement and catch every breeze. This careful gradation from sun-lovers to shade-tolerant plants solves that common border challenge where light levels shift. Everything here is completely hardy and low maintenance once established. The contrast between fiery reds and cool purples creates a buzz, and by staking early in the season, this combination virtually looks after itself, providing structural seed heads right through winter.

***Crocosmia* 'Lucifer'** One of the hardiest montbretias available, with brilliant scarlet-red funnel flowers on arching 1.2m (4ft) stems. This robust perennial also tolerates partial shade better than most of its kind, while the late summer flowering coincides perfectly with *Veronicastrum*. Divide congested clumps every 3–4 years to maintain vigour. **HARDINESS: RHS H5**

***Veronicastrum virginicum* 'Fascination'** Delivering lilac-blue flower spikes like elegant shooting stars on 1.5–1.8m (5–6ft) stems, 'Fascination' occasionally produces fasciated (flattened) flower stems, adding extra interest. Extremely hardy and fairly self-supporting, despite its height, it flowers from midsummer into early autumn, attracting masses of pollinators. **HARDINESS: RHS H7**

Miscanthus sinensis This tall grass brings essential movement to late summer borders. Choose cultivars such as 'Malepartus' (mahogany-red plumes), 'Morning Light' (compact at 1.2m/4ft tall), or 'China' (brownish-pink panicles). All tolerate partial shade better than most ornamental grasses. Leave standing through winter for structure. **HARDINESS: RHS H6**

Matteuccia struthiopteris This deciduous shuttlecock fern creates dramatic vase-like forms at the shadier end. Fresh green sterile fronds reach 1–1.5m (3⅓–5ft), with distinctive brown fertile fronds appearing in late summer. Spreads by underground rhizomes but rarely invasive. Extremely hardy and tolerant of deep shade. Cut back in late winter. **HARDINESS: RHS H7**

TIPS FOR SUCCESS

- Position plants according to light needs: *Crocosmia* in sun, transitioning through *Veronicastrum* to ferns in shade.
- Prepare soil with generous applications of organic matter throughout – all these plants appreciate moisture retention.
- Apply a 5–7.5cm (2–3in) mulch annually to maintain consistent moisture across the transition zone.
- Leave *Miscanthus* and *Veronicastrum* stems standing through winter to add structural interest.

Copper & Amethyst

Naturalistic layers that hum with life

This combination captures everything I love about late summer – that glorious phase when formal meets informal, and the garden takes on a life of its own. I've layered purple spikes and bronze fennel clouds to create a planting that looks effortlessly natural but is anything but accidental.

The magic happens when you mix cottage garden stalwarts with prairie-style perennials, letting them mingle like old friends at a party. Plant this in full sun to light shade and average, well-drained soil, and you'll have a display that peaks from midsummer into early autumn. The predominantly purple palette creates contrast without shouting. I adore the kind of comfortable 'organised chaos'.

Betonica officinalis **'Hummelo'** Garden designer Piet Oudolf's brilliant selection has become the go-to betony for good reason. The 45–60cm (1½–2ft) purple-pink flower spikes rise above neat clumps of crinkled leaves from early to late summer, with the main show in midsummer. Completely bulletproof in sun or partial shade, it spreads gently without being thuggish. The sturdy stems never need staking, and bees absolutely adore it. HARDINESS: RHS H7

Foeniculum vulgare **'Atropurpureum'** Bronze fennel is the ultimate see-through plant, creating 1.8m (6ft) clouds of feathery, copper-purple foliage topped with acid-yellow umbels in late summer. It self-seeds with enthusiasm (consider yourself warned), but those seedlings are easily edited out or relocated. The aromatic edible foliage provides stunning textural contrast, while the flowers support countless beneficial insects. HARDINESS: RHS H5

Echinacea purpurea **'Magnus'** This 1985 introduction by Jelitto Seeds, named in honour of Swedish breeder Magnus B. Nilsson, remains one of the finest purple coneflowers. Its 12cm (5in) rose-purple daisies with prominent orange-bronze cones bloom from midsummer to mid-autumn on sturdy 90cm (3ft) stems. Superior to many newer cultivars for vigour and longevity, 'Magnus' never fails to deliver. Leave seed heads for winter interest and goldfinch fodder. HARDINESS: RHS H5

TIPS FOR SUCCESS

- Plant in groups of 3–5 for impact, allowing adequate spacing for them to mature.
- Deadhead betony after the first flush of flowers for a potential second blooming.
- Allow fennel to self-seed, then thin seedlings as desired in spring.
- Leave all seed heads standing for winter structure and wildlife value.

Foeniculum vulgare 'Atropurpureum'

Betonica officinalis 'Hummelo'

Opposite *Echinacea purpurea* 'Magnus'

Above The late summer mingle where cottage garden meets prairie style

Sunset in the Veg Patch

Late summer's most delicious combination

There's something wonderfully rebellious about this corner of my garden that makes me so happy! I've completely ignored the 'proper' rules about keeping vegetables separate from ornamentals and planted the annual *Ipomoea lobata* (Spanish flag) climber with my favourite peas 'Alderman' in order to make the bean sticks glow with neon blooms.

Add in some fiery *Tagetes* 'Burning Ember' at their feet and let bronze fennel, purple coneflowers and *Verbena bonariensis* weave through the whole glorious muddle to invite the colour and so the pollinators in, which will give you greater vegetable yields.

This is the area I call my 'vegetable splodge' – a patch where flowers for cutting mingle with crops and beauty and productivity refuse to be separated. Plant in full sun with decent soil, and you'll have colour, dinner and wildlife habitat all rolled into one. The sunset colour scheme works because warm oranges and reds play off those cool purples and blues, while everything earns its keep through gorgeous looks, edible bits or sheer usefulness.

TIPS FOR SUCCESS

- Share climbing supports between ornamental and edible vines for maximum space efficiency.
- Water deeply but less frequently in late summer heat – early morning is best.
- Plant marigolds near vegetables as natural pest deterrents.
- Allow bronze fennel and verbena to self-seed, but edit out excess seedlings.
- Harvest peas regularly to keep plants productive through the season.
- Deadhead marigolds and verbena but leave some echinacea heads for birds.

Ipomoea lobata **(Spanish Flag)** This climbing annual is absolutely brilliant, producing those extraordinary flower spikes that open deep red at the base and fade through orange to cream at the tips – like living sunset gradients. Reaching 3–4m (10–13ft), it happily shares support structures with edible climbers, making your bean poles twice as productive. Start seeds indoors in spring warmth, then plant out after frosts in a sunny, sheltered spot. **HARDINESS: RHS H2**

Pisum sativum **'Alderman'** This Victorian heritage cultivar from 1891 produces enormous, curved pods packed with 8–11 sweet, tender peas. The 2m (6½ft) vines are brilliant climbers, happy to share supports with ornamental partners while fixing nitrogen in the soil for neighbouring plants. Sow in early spring for summer crops, or again in midsummer for autumn harvest in milder areas. **HARDINESS: FROST TOLERANT**

Tagetes **'Burning Ember'** These French marigolds earn their place through sheer hard work – those intense mahogany-red blooms edged with gold at up to 50cm tall flower non-stop while their scent may help deter some pests from precious vegetables. The petals are edible too, adding spicy colour to summer salads. **HARDINESS: RHS H2**

Verbena bonariensis The see-through plant that ties everything together with its wiry 1.2-1.5m (4–5ft) stems topped by clusters of lilac-purple flowers. Needs virtually no maintenance once established and bends rather than breaks in autumn gales. **HARDINESS: RHS H4**

Foeniculum vulgare **'Atropurpureum'** (see p.124)
Echinacea purpurea **'Magnus'** (see p.124)

Pisum sativum 'Alderman'

Above *Tagetes* 'Burning Ember' **Opposite** *Ipomoea lobata*

WHAT TO DO
LATE SUMMER

As the garden passes summer's mid-point and light takes on its distinctive golden quality, this transitional period presents both opportunities and challenges. The shift from early summer's exuberance to autumn's approach requires considered intervention – strategic actions that extend seasonal interest while preparing for the months ahead. It's a fascinating phase of the gardening year where careful management can deliver exceptional results through to autumn's finale.

Watering Wisely

Late summer watering demands precision. Deep, infrequent soaks prove far more effective than frequent shallow waterings, wetting the soil or compost in a pot at lower depths and encouraging robust root development that serves plants well, into autumn and the years ahead.

The persistent myth about water droplets burning leaves deserves to be debunked – if a plant shows genuine stress, water immediately regardless of time. However, it's worth noting that many plants exhibit natural midday wilting as a protective mechanism, recovering fully by evening. Experience helps distinguish between genuine drought stress and temporary heat response.

I water either in the early morning or evening – not to prevent leaf burn, but to maximise efficiency and minimise evaporation. Priority should go to recent plantings, containers and specimens clearly showing stress. Established perennials, climbers, shrubs and trees are generally more drought tolerant than you might think.

Creating soil basins around individual plants prevents wasteful runoff, particularly on sloping sites. Applying a 7–10cm (3–4in) mulch layer, kept clear of stems, significantly reduces evaporation while moderating soil temperature – this essential summer maintenance task really pays dividends.

Taking Semi-Ripe Cuttings

Late summer provides ideal conditions for propagating many ornamental plants with semi-hardwood cuttings. This method offers excellent success rates with minimal equipment.

Suitable subjects include *Hydrangea arborescens* 'Annabelle' and other hydrangea species, the butterfly bush (*Buddleja davidii*), mock orange (*Philadelphus* species) and various perennials, such as *Salvia* species, including Russian sage (*Salvia atriplicifolia*) and *Penstemon* cultivars. Morning collection ensures maximum turgidity and the best results – select 10–15cm (4–6in) shoots, where the base has begun to mature while tips remain soft.

The standard way to propagate using this method involves removing the lower leaves, with a couple of sets remaining at the top of the cutting, treating the base of the stem with rooting hormone if you like, and inserting it into a pot of free-draining medium (equal parts horticultural grit and peat-free compost works well). Maintaining humidity under a clear plastic or glass cover, while providing bright, indirect light, typically produces roots within 3–6 weeks.

Renovating Tired Borders

Late summer often reveals gaps and exhausted areas within borders, presenting opportunities for strategic renovation without major upheaval.

Cutting back spent perennials such as *Geranium* species and *Nepeta* × *faassenii* to the base, if you didn't do this earlier, often stimulates fresh foliage and yet more flowering (see also p.100). This rejuvenation technique works particularly well with plants that naturally regenerate from their bases.

Filling gaps with the last of my 'back-up' annuals – *Cosmos bipinnatus*, *Zinnia elegans* and *Nicotiana* cultivars provides last minute late colour. Do a stock-take of your garden and make a note of where late-season perennials such as asters or ornamental grasses might give a bit of extra oomph, adding them to your list for planting in autumn. They will then settle in and be ready to perform next year. And if your lawn is beginning to creep into your borders, use a halfmoon spade or an edging tool to form a crisp line between the two; it's amazing how creating definition instantly improves both your border and the lawn that frames it – a simple but effective technique.

Supporting Heavy Blooms

Prevention proves far more effective than attempting to remedy storm damage, and late summer's mature growth often requires discrete support systems to prevent collapse.

If companion plants aren't acting as natural supports – for example, cosmos threading its way through sturdy perennials by its side – I have a stash of metal half hoops in various sizes ready to go. These are particularly useful for the front of borders where geraniums or other plants might be damaging your grass. A simple hoop driven into the border will lift foliage and flower from the lawn's surface, saving both plant and turf from potential damage.

Collecting seed

Wandering through the garden in late summer, armed with some paper bags, looking for ripe seed heads is one of life's simple pleasures. I love to harvest my own seed from now until mid-autumn, sowing it immediately in pots or trays of seed compost, or storing tender types indoors until spring. Try hardy geraniums, *Echinacea*, gaura (*Oenothera lindheimeri*), *Aquilegia*, *Nigella* and cosmos. If you sow the seed of F_1 hybrids they may not come true to type, often resulting in flowers that look different to the parent, but it's fun to see what develops from these little capsules.

Leave until the seed heads turn brown – you may hear the seeds rattling inside – then snip them off and place in a bag, where they will then release their cargo. Pour the seeds on to a piece of paper and remove any plant debris, before storing in a labelled, airtight container in a cool place until you are ready to sow them.

MY ESSENTIAL DOS AND DON'TS

+ Water thoroughly but less often – your plants will develop wonderfully strong roots.
+ Keep that mulch topped up generously around your plants.
+ Take semi-hardwood cuttings while growth is still vigorous.
+ Get supports in place before autumn storms arrive.
+ Be brave when cutting back tired perennials – they'll reward you with fresh growth.
+ Keep some gap-filling annuals in reserve for instant colour.
+ Feed those hard-working containers every week.
+ Create temporary shade for any plants struggling in extreme heat.
+ Keep wildlife water sources topped up throughout dry spells.
+ Keep a close eye on containers – they really suffer if they dry out completely.

- Use high-nitrogen feeds now – we don't want the soft growth they encourage before winter and frosts that could damage it.
- Prune spring-flowering shrubs – their buds are already forming for next year's blooms and if you do they may be lost.
- Try any heavy pruning that might encourage vulnerable late growth.

Drought Recovery Plan
Easy ways to revive heat-stressed plants

After years of nursing drought-stressed plants back from disaster, I've developed my own approach to bringing plants back to life after they've succumbed to the sun. The secret? Gentle rehabilitation rather than panic watering. Think convalescent care rather than emergency room drama. This method has saved some of my most precious plants during brutal summers.

1 Assess the damage
Inspect plants in the morning. Look for wilting that doesn't recover overnight, crispy leaf edges or slightly pale colouring that signals dehydration. Test the soil at root level by pushing your fingers into the earth, or invest in a moisture metre probe. Crusty surfaces often hide adequate moisture below.

2 Water strategically
Young plants and recent additions top the priority list for watering. Patience is also crucial here. Use the gentlest setting, emulating summer rain, not monsoon. Water in stages: soak first, leave for 30 minutes, then add a second application. For precious specimens, create a temporary moat by making a raised soil ring around the plant. Always water during cool periods – it's midday watering, not leaf burn, that wastes water through evaporation.

3 Provide temporary shade
Get creative with screening – try old net curtains, garden furniture, shade cloth. Position shade where afternoon sun is fiercest. Simply move container plants to a shadier spot. Both strategies give time for roots to absorb water while the leaves aren't losing moisture through transpiration faster than they can replace it.

4 Apply emergency mulch
Any organic material works – compost, bark, even newspaper topped with grass clippings. Spread a layer 7–10cm (3–4in) thick, avoiding direct stem contact. For shrubs, extend the mulch to the drip line (edge of the canopy) where feeding roots are concentrated. This instant insulation moderates soil temperatures and reduces moisture loss dramatically.

5 Adjust nutrition
Resist immediate feeding – stressed roots cannot process nutrients effectively. Wait for new growth, then begin with a quarter-strength liquid all-purpose feed. These gentle tonics provide trace elements without overwhelming damaged root systems. Consider it plant convalescence food.

6 Monitor progress
Make daily checks routine, and maintain moisture levels without waterlogging. New growth typically emerges within two weeks if roots remain viable. Gradually reduce shade as plants strengthen. Some leaf loss is normal – focus on emerging growth rather than lost foliage. Recovery requires patience but usually succeeds.

Annual Display Makeover
Extending summer colour in containers

Late summer containers often look battle-weary – leggy cosmos, threadbare marigolds. But stepping in to intervene when your annual displays look tired can transform them into autumn showstoppers, promoting new growth, more flowers and a fabulous second wind from seemingly exhausted plants.

1 Evaluate current condition
Inspect your plants in morning light to reveal your plants' true challenges. Check the potential of each: healthy roots (use a gentle tug test), signs of basal growth, overall vigour. Some may not be worth rejuvenating and you shouldn't feel guilty about retiring your plant to the compost bin, but many seemingly finished plants can be given a new lease of life.

2 Prune decisively
Steel yourself for dramatic cuts. Reduce leggy growth by one-third to a half – yes, really! They'll look shocking temporarily, then explode with fresh new growth. Remove every spent flower and yellow leaf. It seems harsh but produces remarkable results.

3 Refresh the growing medium
Scrape away the top 5–7cm (2–3in) of depleted compost – usually crusty and lifeless. Replace with fresh compost mixed with slow-release fertiliser. This renovation will reinvigorate root systems dramatically.

4 Feed for flowers
Weekly feeding becomes essential now. Apply a high-potassium tomato feed at half strength to promote flowering over foliage. Supplement this with a foliar feed, using diluted seaweed-based products – stressed plants absorb nutrients efficiently through their leaves. Always feed during cool conditions – morning or evening – to make sure the plant has time to take up the fertiliser.

5 Fill strategic gaps
Replace failures with fresh annuals selected for late performance. Add height in large pots with *Cleome* or *Nicotiana* – evening fragrance included. Group replacements for impact rather than scattered singles. These newcomers provide immediate colour while the pruned plants recover.

6 Maintain momentum
Consistency matters most. Water regularly without drowning – soggy conditions promote leaves over flowers. Continue weekly feeding regardless of temperature drops, and position containers for morning sun and afternoon shade during hot summers. Persistent deadheading also maintains flower production. I can't tell you how immensely rewarding it is to see your plants bounce back to full health.

Early Autumn

As the landscape paints itself in shades of rich gold, deep crimson and burnished bronze, the light changes too, becoming softer and casting long shadows across our garden borders to make the colour more saturated somehow. Early autumn is when we enter a period of glowing abandon, ember blooms accompanied by a fuzz of grasses and spotted with seed heads binding together a scrapbook of the season.

Let's not forget that early autumn marks a season of harvest and abundance. The garden's colours still feel exuberant, but as the dahlias sizzle, there is a palpable shift in their tone. They invite us to pause and savour their riches, the last wave of colour before winter's approach.

Wandering the garden, the air is often crisp and invigorating, carrying the scent of ripening windfall apples and the earthy aroma of just-fallen leaves on rain-soaked earth. It's the time when the garden crescendos with a final floriferous bounty, rewarding our year's work with bold beauty, and I don't like to miss a moment.

In this gentle transition, the garden shares a particular vibrancy born of contrast – fresh blooms against first-turning crisp leaves, cool, misty mornings giving way to warm afternoons. Spider webs draped with dew glisten in the golden light, while seed heads stand tall, their useful architecture suddenly becoming known. A time of simultaneous endings and beginnings, we're invited to contemplate the year as we harvest the last tomatoes while planting spring bulbs.

When planning for early autumn colour, consider creating a tapestry of warm tones that echo the changing leaves. Think burnt oranges, deep reds and golden yellows. Showstopping

Amelanchier foliage painting itself golden as dahlias carry on regardless – this is early autumn's glorious refusal to let summer go completely

perennials, such as the finely quilled ray florets of golden *Rudbeckia subtomentosa* 'Henry Eilers', and the regal, rich purple spires of *Salvia* 'Amistad', form the backbone of my autumn display. I interplant these with the fiery oranges of sunflowers and the deep red to pink blooms of *Cosmos bipinnatus* 'Rubenza' for a truly spectacular show.

Plants that echo the movement of the season play a strong supporting role, with grasses adding a new dimension and texture to your borders, like the chorus in the final act of the late summer display. Ornamental grasses such as *Calamagrostis brachytricha* and *Miscanthus sinensis* 'Malepartus' catch the low autumn light beautifully, while the pink plumes of *Pennisetum orientale* 'Flamingo' provide a stunning contrast to the hotter tones around them. Mixed through other plants, the feathery plumes of grasses add height and a sense of airiness, lifting your borders and catching the light.

Don't be afraid to introduce surprising pops of colour, too. The vivid blue flowers of asters, (or *Symphyotrichum*, *Eurybia*, *Kalimeris* and even *Afroaster*, as many are now called) or the pure white of Japanese anemones, can add a refreshing contrast to the warmer shades.

Also remember that autumn colour isn't just about flowers. The foliage of shrubs or small trees – *Amelanchier* × *lamarckii* and *Sorbus aria* 'Lutescens' in my modest garden – transform into medleys of yellow, orange and ochre, which become living confetti as they drop, fluttering foliage butterflies that rest upon lawns and borders, bringing in colour of their own. Make sure you have plenty of late-flowering bulbs like the autumn crocus, *Colchicum autumnale* or *Cyclamen hederifolium* to create another layer of joyful colour clashes as they emerge

The irresistible *Rudbeckia subtomentosa* 'Henry Eilers' **(top)**; *Miscanthus sinensis* 'Malepartus' and *Pennisetum orientale* 'Flamingo' catching the light **(bottom)**

through fallen leaves – always a joyous discovery to chance upon in any garden.

For dramatic autumn accents, I incorporate shrubs with colourful berries and stems that create talking points. Following the flowers, these jewel-like fruits become the garden's seasonal treasures. The vivid berries of the new beautyberry, *Callicarpa* PEARL GLAM, which has bead-like purple fruits for many months throughout autumn and winter, and young ruby red leaves for border presence earlier in the year, or *Viburnum opulus* 'Xanthocarpum', a spectacular form of our native guelder rose, its autumn clusters of golden yellow, almost translucent, berries lasting well into the winter before finally feeding the birds. These are mixed with the first hints of colour in *Cornus* stems, creating vertical shards of orange, plum or scarlet, and sometimes all three.

Keeping everything blooming for as long as possible (and to allow me more time outdoors) becomes of paramount

Early autumn residents – *Anemone hupehensis* var. *japonica* 'Pamina' providing late colour **(left)**; while garden spiders move in, weaving their own contribution to the season's texture **(right)**

The key to creating a garden rich in autumnal colour is to consider it as a tapestry. Think texture, form and movement as essential threads to stitch together.

importance at this time of year. I become a deadheading obsessive! Armed with secateurs, I move through the garden each evening, removing the spent flower heads of late-flowering perennials and annuals. That said, hold off on major cutbacks until later – many seed heads provide food and shelter for wildlife and glittering architectural interest through the winter.

But that's still a while away yet. For now, take time to lie in your hammock or pull up a chair among the last blaze's ebb, flicking through your garden pictures to assess summer's successes and failures, making notes while memories are fresh, and planning next year's adjustments.

As you plan, remember that this is an excellent time for establishing new plants. The soil is still warm, encouraging root growth, while increased rainfall reduces the need for watering. Then there are the spring-flowering bulbs to bury in the earth or plant into pots (always a marathon for me!), overgrown perennials to divide, and plants to be moved around to better positions. More on all this later.

Ultimately, I think the key to creating a garden rich in autumnal colour is to consider it as a tapestry. Think texture, form and movement as essential threads to stitch together. Textural variety, dynamic colour contrasts and layers of different heights all contribute to a scene that feels full of life and movement.

With the right choices, early autumn becomes not a time of winding down, but rather a breathtaking crescendo – a moment where the garden takes on a new kind of brilliance, glowing warmly even as the first chills of the impending winter begin to whisper.

Sparkling Performers
Airy grasses combined with bold annual blooms

Blending delicate textures with bold blooms, the annuals *Zinnia elegans* 'Queen Lime Red' and *Cosmos bipinnatus* 'Apricotta' provide pops of warm colour at this time of year, while *Dahlia* 'Bright Eyes' and *Trifolium rubens* offer a focal point in the foreground. The airy plumes of *Panicum* 'Sprinkles' add an ethereal quality to the arrangement, bringing the colours and textures together. For all annuals, I adore experimenting with the tones and textures of different varieties to create ephemeral displays that change every year.

This grouping thrives in full sun and well-drained, fertile soil, and the flowers will continue to bloom through until the first frosts if you keep on top of deadheading.

Panicum **'Sprinkles'** This diaphanous grass, reaching 60–90cm (2–3ft) in height, produces hair-fine sprays of light, airy, pale green flowers that resemble sparklers when lit by the sun. This super easy-to-grow half-hardy annual needs to be surface sown in spring, and the seedlings then transplanted in clumps into individual pots, before planting out after all danger of frost has passed. You'll find it self-seeds too. HARDINESS: RHS H4

Zinnia elegans **'Queen Lime Red'** I adore the individuality of the striking Queen series of zinnias, each variety a blend of exquisite vintage tones. A unique lime green and deep rose, 'Queen Lime Red' produces double flowers on sturdy stems about 60–75cm (2–2½ft) tall, providing not just bold colour and structure to plant arrangements, but continuous blooms from midsummer until the frosts in autumn. HARDINESS: RHS H2

Cosmos bipinnatus **'Apricotta'** Complementing the *Zinnia* perfectly, with burnished apricot and peach petals, this tall annual reaches 1–1.2m (3–4ft) in height. The delicate, ferny foliage swirls around its companions, adding a dreamy, cottage-garden feel to the planting, while the flowers appear from midsummer to autumn. HARDINESS: RHS H3

Dahlia **'Bright Eyes'** A new favourite of mine, this single-flowered cultivar produces masses of vibrant, purple-pink blooms, each with a cream-yellow heart, that attract pollinators from summer to the first frosts. Reaching a height of around 1m (3ft), the dusky foliage is also attractive and offers a contrast to a host of companion plants. HARDINESS: RHS H3

Trifolium rubens (see p.113)

TIPS FOR SUCCESS

- Plant in well-drained, moderately fertile soil.
- Provide full sun for best flowering, though light shade is tolerated.
- Space plants generously to allow for natural growth and movement.
- Deadhead zinnias, cosmos and dahlias regularly to prolong flowering.
- Leave seed heads of *Panicum* standing for winter interest and wildlife value.
- Sow *Panicum* 'Sprinkles' in succession for a continuous supply of stems.
- Consider using *Panicum* 'Sprinkles' as a dried flower for extended seasonal interest in your home.
- Water consistently, especially during dry spells, to maintain soil moisture and promote healthy growth.

Cosmos bipinnatus 'Apricotta' and *Trifolium rubens* **(top left)**; *Zinnia elegans* 'Queen Lime Red' stands tall **(top right)**; *Dahlia* 'Bright Eyes' pops its head into view top right while the feathery *Panicum* 'Sprinkles' can be seen bottom left **(bottom)**

Quilled Sunshine & Purple Haze

Dynamic textures and colours for early autumn impact

As summer fades, this energetic combination brings a fresh burst of life to the garden. The quilled petals of *Rudbeckia subtomentosa* 'Henry Eilers' create a starry display of golden yellow, which is perfectly complemented by the rich purple spikes of *Verbena × baileyana* 'Purple Haze'. These colours sit opposite one another on the colour wheel, creating a vibrant tension that makes each appear more intense – nature's perfect colour theory in action.

Beyond their visual appeal, these complementary hues create high contrast that pollinators adore. Bees and butterflies navigate easily between the golden stars and purple clouds, extending the garden's ecological value deep into autumn. The airy inflorescences of *Deschampsia cespitosa* 'Goldtau' add a third dimension, catching the low seasonal light, while at the same time creating misty movement that softens the structural blooms.

Plant in generous drifts, allowing the verbena to thread its way through the upright rudbeckia, while the grasses dance between them. This textural tapestry thrives in full sun to partial shade, creating a breathtaking finale that continues to nourish both wildlife and the gardener's soul as days grow shorter.

Rudbeckia subtomentosa **'Henry Eilers'** This stand-out coneflower carries unique spindles of liquorice-scented yellow petals surrounding a central orange-brown cone. Growing to 1.2–1.5m (4–5ft) tall, it forms self-supporting, sturdy clumps with softly hairy, sweetly aromatic foliage. Flowers appear from late summer to autumn, providing a long season of interest and valuable late nectar for pollinators.
HARDINESS: RHS H6

Verbena × baileyana **'Purple Haze'** A long-flowering, branching, dark-leaved perennial, this hybrid is a cross between *V. officinalis* 'Bampton' and *V. hastata* f. *rosea*, and gives the popular *V. bonariensis* a run for its money in the flowering stakes. Very attractive to pollinators, the plant reaches about a metre (3ft) in height, its rich purple flower clusters appearing from midsummer to late autumn, creating a hazy effect in the border. Grow in moist but well-drained, moderately fertile soil in full sun, though it will take a smidge of shade.
HARDINESS: RHS H5

Deschampsia cespitosa **'Goldtau'** Thriving in both sun and light shade, this superbly versatile, mound-forming evergreen grass produces elegant clumps of fine, dark green leaves, topped with airy panicles of silvery, reddish-brown flower spikes in midsummer, which turn a lovely warm buff in autumn and persist well into winter. Growing to around 1m (3ft) in height, it adds movement and texture to plantings. This adaptable plant is laid back about where it grows, and will be happy in moist soil, clay, loam, and sand.
HARDINESS: RHS H5

TIPS FOR SUCCESS

- Space plants generously to allow for natural growth and movement.
- Deadhead rudbeckia regularly to prolong flowering.
- Leave seed heads and grass plumes standing for winter interest and wildlife value.
- Divide clumps every 3–4 years in spring to maintain their vigour and prevent overcrowding.

Container Crescendo

A potted palette of dahlias with Thalictrum *backdrop*

Bringing together the rich, varied tones of dahlias in pots, *Thalictrum* 'Elin' is planted in the borders behind to create a stunning late summer to early autumn display, its colours evolving as the weeks pass to create a chameleon-like backdrop. Although many people consider only the flower colour of dahlias, it's important to think about the foliage, too. The dark leaves of *Dahlia* 'Waltzing Mathilda' draw attention to the display, announcing that they're here to command your view, while echoing the bronze-flushed foliage of *Dahlia* 'Bishop of Canterbury'. The apricot pink and gold-flushed autumn foliage of the *Thalictrum* ties in with the flower colours of the dahlias, those with single blooms drawing in the pollinators, while the larger, attention-grabbing heads of *Dahlia* 'Labyrinth' adding bulk to the scene. Varying heights and textures of both the pots and dahlias planted within them create a layered effect, perfect for patios or prominent spots in the garden.

Thalictrum **'Elin'** A statuesque perennial reaching up to 2.5m (8ft), its attractive blue-grey foliage tinged with purple bubbling from the earth in spring before producing myriad airy sprays of dusky lavender-pink flowers in summer. Less often discussed, the technicolour autumn tones are sensational, perfect for creating wonderful associations with many plants at this time of year. HARDINESS: RHS H7

Dahlia **'Waltzing Mathilda'** Perhaps my favourite dahlia, its deep black-purple foliage giving rise to warm, coral-pink flowers with hints of red and orange, each large, single bloom featuring a slight twist in the petal from late summer into autumn. Did you know that all dahlia petals are edible, too? The more you cut, the more they bloom, both perfect excuses to bring the flowers indoors. This pollinator favourite grows to around 60cm (2ft) tall, providing a rich contrast to many potential companions. HARDINESS; RHS H3

Dahlia **'Labyrinth'** Huge, shaggy, double blooms in a mouthwatering blend of twirling peachy orange and dark pink. This flamboyant dahlia reaches around 1m (3ft) in height, making it perfect for a starring role in a pot and a bold centrepiece for any home-grown flower arrangement. HARDINESS: RHS H3

Dahlia **'Bishop of Canterbury'** Magenta pink-purple flowers create a vivid contrast with the bronze-flushed foliage from midsummer onwards. The generous numbers of single blooms act as a beacon for bees and other pollinating insects. Growing to just under 1m (3ft) tall, it provides a strong central focus and adds depth to the overall colour palette. HARDINESS: RHS H3

> **TIPS FOR SUCCESS**
> - Use large, deep containers to accommodate the root systems of these vigorous dahlias.
> - Ensure excellent drainage by adding grit to the potting mix.
> - Feed regularly with a potassium-rich fertiliser to encourage abundant flowering.
> - Deadhead dahlias frequently to promote continuous blooming.
> - Provide sturdy support for the tall *Thalictrum* 'Elin'.
> - In mid-autumn, either move pots to a frost-free location, or lift and store the dahlia tubers in a dry, frost-free place or, if growing in borders, protect with thick mulch.
> - Water pots consistently, especially during dry spells, to maintain moisture levels in the compost.

Dahlia 'Labyrinth'

Dahlia 'Waltzing Mathilda'

Opposite *Dahlia* 'Bishop of Canterbury' with *Dahlia* 'Waltzing Mathilda'

Above Peak dahlia season in pots – *this* is why I grow them!

Fading Glory

Celebrating the beauty of early autumn's seed heads

This energetic combination captures late summer transitioning into autumn, showcasing a variety of textures and forms. I've always adored watching the lives of plants as they change, having something of the Miss Havisham about me. Here, the arching plumes of *Miscanthus sinensis* 'Malepartus' create movement, while the architectural seed heads of the teasel, *Dipsacus laciniatus*, add structural interest and a contrast of shape. In the foreground, the soft, fuzzy foliage of *Pennisetum orientale* 'Flamingo' provides a delicate softness, echoing the towering *Eutrochium purpureum* in the background. This grouping thrives in full sun to partial shade, and prefers well-drained soil. Plant in generous drifts for maximum impact, allowing the grasses to weave through the more upright perennials. The combination offers visual interest from late summer through winter, with the addition of the sunflower *Helianthus annuus* 'Red Sun' and *Thalictrum* 'Elin' just out of shot, extending the colour palette.

> **TIPS FOR SUCCESS**
> - Plant in well-drained, moderately fertile soil, apart from the *Eutrochium*, which needs more moisture than the others.
> - Provide full sun for best flowering, though light shade is tolerated by these plants, too.
> - Allow ample space for plants to reach their full size and create natural drifts.
> - Leave seed heads and grass plumes standing for winter interest and wildlife value.
> - Cut back *Miscanthus* and *Pennisetum* to the ground in late winter, just as the new growth begins to emerge.
> - Divide clumps every 3–4 years to maintain your plants' vigour and prevent overcrowding.

***Miscanthus sinensis* 'Malepartus'** A statuesque grass reaching 2m (6½ft) in height, its arching green leaves featuring white midribs give upthrust and vertical lift to the combination. I adore this *Miscanthus* variety, primarily because of its unusual deep burgundy flower plumes, which emerge in late summer and become buff feathers as they mature, providing excellent summer colour, autumn texture and winter structure. **HARDINESS: RHS H6**

Dipsacus laciniatus This biennial plant forms leafy rosettes in its first year, followed by flower stems up to 2m (6½ft) tall in the second year. The distinctive, spherical flower heads contain hundreds of tiny cream blooms with contrasting reddish stamens, and emerge from prickly stems above deeply cut, jagged leaves, before maturing into sculptural seed heads that add vertical interest and wildlife value to the garden. Every pair of leaves forms a cup where it joins the stem, which often collects water for wildlife, while the flowers provide pollen for bumblebees, large moths and butterflies, and small birds and mammals eat the seeds in autumn and winter. Be warned, it self-seeds readily but is easy to dig out when young. **HARDINESS: RHS H7**

***Pennisetum orientale* 'Flamingo'** A beautiful fountain grass growing to around 75cm (2½ft) tall, with upright arching leaves and soft, pink, bottle brush-like flowers from summer to autumn. It's fine-texture adds a delicate, hazy effect to planting schemes and it can helpfully withstand winter temperatures down to around -5°C (23°F). **HARDINESS: RHS H3**

Eutrochium purpureum Formerly known as *Eupatorium*, this sensational perennial's stout stems reach 1.5-2m (5–6½ft) in height bearing large, domed clusters of tiny, cinnamon-pink flowers in late summer, attracting butterflies and providing a strong vertical element. Perfect for damp borders or pond edges. **HARDINESS: RHS H3**

Late Bloomers & Evergreen Elegance

Colour and interest from late-season flowers and cool foliage

The Japanese anemone 'Pamina' takes centre stage in this group, its vibrant purple-pink blooms creating a focal point of generous colour in the border at the end of the summer and into early autumn. *Teucrium hircanicum* 'Paradise Delight' adds depth and texture, its green-purple spikes in the foreground reaching up to tickle the open, happy anemone blooms. Never underestimate foliage as a backdrop to frame a combination. Evergreen *Trachelospermum jasminoides* provides a lush layer at the end of the year, its glossy foliage promising a vibrant red display as temperatures cool. Dark-leaved dahlias in the foreground offer structural contrast and a haze of complementary colour. This grouping thrives in full sun to partial shade, preferring well-drained, fertile soil. Allowing the lower-growing plants to weave between the taller specimens creates an untamed looseness that offers visual interest from late summer through to the first frosts, with the *Trachelospermum* extending interest well into winter.

Anemone hupehensis var. *japonica* **'Pamina'**
One of the older varieties of Japanese anemone, *'Pamina'* is deservedly popular for its sumptuous, large, deep-pink double flowers, each with a golden-yellow centre. It's a shorter-growing anemone, reaching 60–90cm (2–3ft) in height, and its upright habit and profuse blooms make it an excellent choice for the middle of a border. It will happily grow in any garden soil, but avoid excessive winter wet. It can spread rapidly once established, but sometimes that's a good thing, right? **HARDINESS: RHS H7**

Teucrium hircanicum **'Paradise Delight'**
The Caucasian germander is a reliable self-supporting perennial which should be used more. It produces finger-like spires of blooms; lime green in bud, the rosy-purple flowers open progressively from the bottom to the top, rather like a firework. Compact and bushy, with aromatic evergreen grey-green leaves, it offers a soft, textural element, while the flowers, which persist from late summer into early autumn, attract a host of bees and butterflies. **HARDINESS: RHS H6**

Trachelospermum jasminoides An indispensable evergreen twining climber, the star jasmine produces clusters of small, honey-scented, star-shaped white flowers from mid- to late summer. However, it's actually the foliage I grow it for, the glossy, dark green leaves creating the perfect backdrop to any border. In autumn and winter, these turn a vibrant bronze-red, and are a spectacle in themselves. It can take a while to settle into a new position but once content, it sprawls with abandon, which is why I train it horizontally on wires to camouflage fences and offer an excellent backdrop to my borders. **HARDINESS: RHS H4**

Dahlia **(dark-leaved varieties)** Various dahlia cultivars with dark foliage add structural interest and colour contrast in the foreground. These tender plants typically bloom from midsummer until the first frosts, offering a range of flower forms and colours to complement all colour schemes. **HARDINESS: RHS H3**

TIPS FOR SUCCESS

- Plant in well-drained, fertile soil, that is rich in organic matter.
- Provide full sun for the best flowering and autumn colour, though light shade is tolerated.
- Water regularly during the first growing season to establish deep root systems.
- Mulch annually with well-rotted compost to improve soil structure and fertility.
- Deadhead anemones and dahlias regularly to prolong flowering.
- Prune *Trachelospermum* in late winter or early spring to maintain its shape and size.
- Lift and store dahlia tubers in winter if you live in a cold area with harsh frosts.
- Consider providing support for taller dahlias to prevent wind damage.

Beads & Seeds

Graceful seed heads and golden blooms to catch the light

I adore the way the burgundy bobbles of *Sanguisorba officinalis* hover on delicate wiry stems, appearing to float above the feathery plumes of the Korean feather reed grass, *Calamagrostis brachytricha*. *Helianthus annuus* 'Ring of Fire' extends the season's warmth with a cheerful splash of sunny yellow, while the domed, mauve clusters of *Eutrochium purpureum* offer a soft backdrop with volume and height.

Plant this combination in moisture-retentive but well-drained soil in full sun to light shade, where it will provide interest from late summer through autumn until the first hard frosts. The airy, light textures of the bouncing seed heads and fluffy grass plumes look especially wonderful when backlit, so consider where to plant them for the best effect. For different soil types, consider adding *Molinia caerulea* subsp. *arundinacea* 'Transparent' in drier conditions or *Vernonia noveboracensis* for heavier clay.

Sanguisorba officinalis This elegant perennial showcases distinctive, burgundy, button-like flower heads on slender, wiry stems that dance in the slightest breeze. Growing to 1.2m (4ft) tall, great burnet provides vertical interest and textural contrast from mid-summer to mid-autumn. It grows in most soils, but prefers moist, well-drained soil in full sun or partial shade, and the flowers attract a wealth of pollinators. **HARDINESS: RHS H7**

Helianthus annuus **'Ring of Fire'** This hardy sunflower forms branching stems of flame-yellow flowers with dark centres from late summer into autumn. Reaching 1.5m (5ft) in height, it creates a sunny backdrop to this group, complementing its cooler-toned companions. Happy in well-drained soil in full sun, it's a magnet for bees and butterflies. **HARDINESS: RHS H4**

Calamagrostis brachytricha Korean feather reed grass forms neat clumps of arching foliage topped with fountains of feathery, pinkish-silver plumes. These open in late summer and early autumn and persist into the winter fading to buff as autumn progresses. Reaching 1.2m (4ft) in height, it brings movement and catches light beautifully. Versatile and unfussy, it performs well in most soils in sun or partial shade. **HARDINESS: RHS H6**

Eutrochium purpureum (see p. 157)

> **TIPS FOR SUCCESS**
> - Leave the seed heads of perennials and grasses to remain standing through winter for structural interest and wildlife habitat; cut them back in late winter.
> - Rejuvenate *Sanguisorba* and *Eutrochium* by dividing them every 3–4 years in spring to maintain their vigour and prevent their centres becoming woody.
> - Place support rings or stakes around the tall plants in late spring before they reach their full height to prevent flopping later in the season.
> - Deadhead *Helianthus annuus* 'Ring of Fire' regularly to encourage continuous blooming throughout the late summer and autumn.
> - Add late-flowering alliums such as 'Summer Drummer' for additional textural interest and pollinator appeal.

EARLY AUTUMN
WHAT TO DO

Early autumn brings gentler temperatures, mellow light and the first blush of colour in deciduous trees. While this shift signals the beginning of summer's end, thankfully, there is still an abundance of blooms in our gardens. Early autumn also marks the beginning of a new gardening season – a perfect time for reflection, preparation and planting. These amber-tinted weeks offer ideal conditions for establishing plants and setting the stage for next year's colourful display.

Sowing for Success

Autumn presents an opportunity to sow hardy annuals and biennials for a head start on next year's display. Plants from autumn sowings typically develop into taller, more robust specimens that flower nearly a month earlier than their spring-sown counterparts. Reliable choices include *Ammi majus*, cornflowers (*Centaurea cyanus*), love-in-a-mist (*Nigella*), larkspur (*Consolida ajacis*), poppies (*Papaver somniferum*), pot marigolds (*Calendula*) and ornamental grasses such as foxtail barley (*Hordeum jubatum*) and quaking grass (*Briza media*).

For best results, sow in trays or modules rather than directly into the ground. This approach provides you with greater control over the growing environment and produces large plants that are less vulnerable to slug damage when finally planted out. Small seeds work well in seed trays of peat-free seed compost, while larger ones can go directly into modules.

Protect young seedlings by placing trays into larger seed trays with clear propagator lids. Position them in an unheated greenhouse, cold frame, bright porch or sheltered spot as temperatures drop. Monitor trays set outdoors after rainfall and tip away any excess water to prevent the seedlings becoming waterlogged.

Extending the Flowering Season

Don't surrender to autumn too readily. The constant deadheading of roses, dahlias and other late-summer bloomers continues to encourage further flowering. Pair this with a liquid feed for your annuals and you're doing all you can to encourage an encore performance of blooms.

When it comes to feeding, I favour my own home-grown wormery fertiliser or a potassium-rich organic fertiliser for a late-season boost. I feed my containers and annuals every Friday and don't intend to stop until I've squeezed every last bloom from my garden. This routine honestly makes a huge difference to the quantity of blooms.

Dividing Perennials

The cooler weather makes this an ideal time for dividing perennials. The damp conditions reduce compaction, allowing us to dig up and split a plant's roots more easily than when the soil is dry and hard during summer, particularly if you garden on clay. It's worth lifting and splitting perennials that have become overcrowded or are underperforming into smaller chunks and then replanting the healthy sections to reinvigorate them, ready to better play their part in next year's display. Suitable candidates include agapanthus, anemones, asters, crocosmia,

hardy geraniums, geums, daylilies (*Hemerocallis*), ornamental grasses and salvias.

The division process is straightforward:
1. Lift plants carefully with a garden fork.
2. Remove excess soil to expose the roots.
3. Divide the rootball using a sharp knife or spade (I use an old pruning saw kept for this purpose).
4. Add a layer of peat-free compost to your planting holes, then replant divisions immediately.
5. Water thoroughly and monitor for slug activity around any fresh new growth.

It's amazing how division rejuvenates tired plants and provides new ones to fill gaps or share with gardening friends.

Training Climbing Plants

While plants remain in leaf, prune any dead or diseased growth and train the strong new shoots of your climbing roses and woody climbers on to their supports.

To achieve fuller coverage and more abundant flowering, train stems horizontally on wires or in gentle curves, rather than vertically. Attach the plant securely, tying your twine in a knot around the wire, then using the ends to make another knot around the stem, so that it doesn't wave about in the wind and snap. Training stems horizontally like this encourages blooming along their entire stem rather than just at the tips. The promise of more flowers has got to make getting out there with the secateurs and garden twine worth it!

Soil Improvement

Great gardens start with great soil and as plants finally begin to fade, it pays dividends to focus attention on enhancing it – one of the most consequential yet frequently overlooked gardening activities. It's time to empty your compost bin and use the finished compost, before beginning the whole process again. Apply a 5cm (2in) layer of your well-rotted compost or manure to your beds, working it gently around existing perennials without smothering their crowns. Worms will then incorporate the organic material into the soil throughout winter, improving its structure, drainage and fertility. As leaves fall, brush them onto your flower beds to decompose as nature intended. These simple tasks will provide your plants with the foundation they need for vigorous growth.

Planning for Spring

If you haven't ordered spring bulbs already, do not delay! Choose a selection that will provide a long show, starting with early bloomers such as snowdrops and crocuses, progressing to daffodils for mid-spring, and finishing with later-flowering varieties such as tulips, fritillaries, alliums and camassias. Also and make a note in your diary to order autumn crocuses and nerines next spring to keep the show going.

While most bulbs can be planted from early autumn onwards, delay tulip planting until later in the season to reduce the risk of tulip fire disease. For container displays, consider the layered 'bulb lasagne' technique (see p.166), which creates sequential waves of blooms from a single container.

MY ESSENTIAL DOS AND DON'TS

+ Collect seeds from open-pollinated favourite flowers on dry days and store in labelled paper envelopes.
+ Create wildlife habitats by leaving log piles or undisturbed corners for hibernating insects, hedgehogs and amphibians.
+ Remove fallen leaves from ponds to prevent them decaying and contaminating the water.
+ Begin forcing bulbs such as paperwhites and amaryllis indoors.
+ Move tender plants under cover before the first frost.
+ Take cuttings from tender perennials as insurance against winter losses.
+ Bring the outdoors inside: cut the last of summer's blooms to enjoy indoors.
+ Renovate your lawn, overseeding bare patches with an appropriate grass seed mix for your specific conditions.

− Cut back all perennials – leave some dried leaves and seed heads for wildlife and winter structure.
− Prune spring-flowering shrubs now or you'll remove next year's blooms.
− Rush to trim hedges. Consider waiting until early winter if you want material for Christmas decorations.
− Ignore your greenhouse: early autumn is the ideal time for a thorough clean (especially before bringing in tender plants for winter), removing shading, checking for repairs and washing glass.

Making a Bulb Lasagne
Create a sparkling spring bulb display in one large pot

Winter is certainly on the horizon, but planting up a container of spring-flowering bulbs now is an act of optimism that your future self will thank you for. There's something deeply satisfying about tucking these dormant treasures into soil or compost before the dark days hit, knowing they'll burst forth with life-affirming colour right when you need it most. A layered bulb planting requires minimal effort, but promises months of bright, mood-lifting blooms from late winter onwards.

1 Prepare your container
Choose a large container, at least 30cm (1ft) deep and wide. Ensure it has drainage holes in the base, then cover these with crocks (broken pot pieces). Add a 5cm (2in) layer of gravel at the bottom to improve drainage, followed by peat-free multipurpose compost, filling approximately one-third of the container.

2 Plant the bottom layer
Position your largest flowering bulbs (typically tulips) at this deepest level. Place them pointed-end up, close together, but not touching. Cover with another layer of compost so you can just see the tips of the bulbs.

3 Add the middle layer
Plant mid-season flowerers such as narcissi in this layer, positioning them in the gaps between the bulbs below. Cover with another layer of compost.

4 Place the top layer
Add early flowering bulbs such as crocuses or dwarf irises. These late winter bloomers will be the first to emerge, kickstarting your display. Cover with compost, leaving about 5cm (2in) between the surface and rim of the pot for a layer of grit and to hold water, so it soaks into the pot and doesn't just spill over the sides.

5 Include winter interest
Plant cold-tolerant bedding plants such as pansies on the surface for immediate colour. Position the flowers evenly, taking care not to dislodge the bulbs below, to create a living mulch that protects while providing winter interest.

6 Finish with grit
Apply a generous layer of decorative grit around the pansies. This deters pests, prevents mud splash on to the flowers and gives a professional finish.

Bulb Selection Tip: The largest, latest-flowering bulbs go deepest, while the smallest, earliest bloomers sit highest. A 30cm (1ft) diameter container can accommodate approximately 30 bulbs across all layers.

Aftercare Tip: Keep compost moist but not waterlogged. As each layer finishes flowering, deadhead spent blooms but allow the foliage to die back naturally, feeding the bulbs for next year's display.

Moving Plants
Early autumn is the best time to relocate plants

Early autumn is the ideal time to move plants, while the soil is warm, and plants have not died down for the winter and are still visible. Moving perennials and ornamental grasses now gives them time to establish fresh roots before winter, ensuring they'll perform better next season in exactly the position you want them.

1 Prepare the new site
Dig a hole slightly larger than the plant's anticipated root ball, placing the excavated soil into a trug. Sprinkle mycorrhizal fungi around the sides and base of the hole to promote healthy root establishment and reduce transplant shock.

2 Bundle the foliage
Gather the plant stems together and secure with garden twine, working from bottom to top. This creates a more manageable shape that protects the crown and prevents damage to both the plant and you during the moving process.

3 Lift carefully
After watering thoroughly the previous day, use a sharp spade to cut around the plant, maintaining as much of the root system as possible. Carefully lift the entire clump, supporting the roots to minimise stress.

4 Position correctly
Place the plant at the same soil depth as its original growing position. This ensures the crown sits correctly in relation to surface and isn't buried beneath wet soil over winter, which may cause rot – critical for your plant's long-term health in its new location.

5 Backfill and firm
Use the soil from your trug to fill in around the roots, gently firming as you go to eliminate air pockets without compacting it. Creating good root-to-soil contact improves the likelihood of establishment success while maintaining necessary drainage.

6 Water and maintain
Remove the protective twine, then water your transplant thoroughly, creating a small basin with a raised ring of soil around the plant to direct moisture to the roots. Continue watering regularly for several weeks if conditions remain dry.

> **Seasonal Tip:** Transplanting in early autumn allows plants to establish before winter without the need for additional fertiliser or compost, which may stimulate unwanted late growth that's vulnerable to frost damage. Leave foliage intact, even if it turns brown, to provide some winter protection before you remove it in early spring to make way for new growth.

Late Autumn

The last of the leaves loosen their grip and spiral downwards as late autumn arrives with a quieter, more introspective beauty. The garden, now subdued, offers a masterclass in the art of letting go. While early autumn blazes with harvest hues, late autumn whispers of survival, endurance and the subtle charms of a landscape preparing for its winter slumber. It's a season I find deeply restorative, a time to connect with the rhythms of nature as the garden simplifies, seems to breathe out and then finally relaxes.

I've always treasured these weeks for their quiet beauty. While many gardeners turn their attention indoors, I find myself drawn outside even more, wrapped in layers against the chill, cup of tea in hand. The garden now reveals its flip side, showing us what has longevity and the staying power to sustain us when the fleeting froth of summer blooms has gone.

Despite the shortening days, the late autumn garden need not lack colour or interest. With thoughtful planning, this season offers some of the most beautiful moments in the gardening calendar, when fragility, form and plants' ephemerality create a palette that's both subtle and surprisingly rich.

The trick is to embrace the muted tones and textures as the plants bleach, fade and ultimately drift away. At this time of year, I'm drawn to dusky purples, turmeric golds, rusty oranges and the buff tones of ornamental grasses. These colours evoke a sense of melancholic beauty, mirroring the fading light and the softening landscape, offering a fragility that's accentuated by the first of the frosts.

For reliable flower power in these waning days, certain plants deserve pride of place. The deep purple spires of *Salvia* 'Amistad'

Bundled up but still pottering – late autumn's quiet beauty is worth braving the weather for

and dahlias often persist well into late autumn, their intense colours creating striking contrasts against the bleached tones around them. These pair beautifully with the architectural seed heads of *Phlomis russeliana*, the garden's drumsticks beating for attention on cold mornings as frost clings to their tiered whorls.

One of my favourite late autumn showstoppers is *Anemone × hybrida* 'Honorine Jobert', its huge, open, white flowers slicing through the day, the nectar-rich blooms a magnet for late-flying insects. The architectural presence of *Baptisia* 'Dutch Chocolate' peppered through my borders adds another layer of interest, with seed heads like baubles in bleached shades of buff and brown. The deep purple spikes of *Salvia uliginosa* also offer a bolt of icy blue before the frost takes it.

Tall grasses become essential players in this seasonal plantscape – *Miscanthus* varieties hold their feathery plumes high against a backdrop of turning leaves, while the more delicate *Pennisetum* catches even the weakest sunlight in its transparent seed heads. I plant these in groups where low winter sunlight will backlight them, creating living sculptures that shift with the slightest breeze.

Of course, approaches to planting design shift with a garden's size and setting. In smaller urban gardens, focus on vertical interest that makes use of the never-ending vertical axis, and containers that can be planted especially for the season to create impact. For rural gardens with sweeping views, larger drifts of grasses and seed heads catch the amber light and move dramatically in autumn winds. I take a different approach for coastal gardens, utilising salt-tolerant structural evergreens, underplanted with late-flowering perennials, protected there from cutting winds.

The trick is to embrace the muted tones and textures as the plants bleach, fade and ultimately drift away

When texture takes over from flowers – late autumn borders proving that seed heads and grasses matter just as much as blooms

The mellow terracotta of containers, mixed with deep ink tones and rusted weathered steel, take on new importance now, their warm tones complementing the season's palette. I cluster pots near doorways and paths where they'll be seen each time I step outside, filling them with bulbs topped with pansies, violas, wallflowers and grit, and giving me much pleasure as I strain to see what's brave enough to venture forth from them during the darkest months.

In my own modest plot, it's a potted ornamental olive tree (*Olea europaea*) in a large urn by the kitchen door that keeps my interest alive at this time of year. Evergreen, with fine, silvery leaves, it provides a structural anchor on my deck year-round, steadfast and upright, looking over a sea of tawny seed heads beyond. This strategic placement near the house transforms the view from my kitchen window during the months when outdoor time becomes more limited.

As we tend our late autumn gardens, there's a delicious interplay between clearing and leaving be, a design choice in itself. I deliberately leave the spent flower heads of echinaceas, gladioli, eryngiums and teasels (*Dipsacus laciniatus*) to stand proud through the cooler months, selectively cutting back only what looks truly spent, while keeping the upright stems of architectural perennials. The seed heads not only become focal points when dusted with frost, or occasionally snow, but provide food for garden birds and winter hotels, where insects hibernate through the coldest months of the

Teasels, grasses and *Eupatorium* seed heads mingling – late autumn's natural bird feeder looking beautiful while serving a purpose

Spring bulbs tucked into pots like presents to open later – late autumn's investment in future colour

year. The goldfinches that delight in picking through teasels become welcome visitors on grey days, their specialised beaks perfectly adapted to extract seeds from the prickly heads. These moments of ephemeral beauty bring the garden to life, even as it seems to be resting.

This season also invites us to secure our plantings for next year, lifting dahlias and bringing them indoors if you live in a cold area, and grouping other slightly tender plants together in a sheltered spot near the house, so that all survive the cold months that lie ahead.

The late autumn garden teaches us patience and appreciation for subtle beauty, but also offers the excitement of anticipation. It reminds us that gardens aren't just about flamboyant flowers, but about texture, structure and the quiet drama of a seed head outlined against a late autumn sky. It's appreciating the small stuff and savouring every moment, as we watch the fading of plants echoing the low light as the year draws to its close.

A Fond Farewell

Celebrating the last of the year's herbs and perennials

In a corner of my deck, the last gasp of my dark-leaved basil is just one example of late autumn's determined beauty, its fragrant leaves, which adorned countless salads and pasta dishes, now standing in dignified retreat. I've deliberately positioned this pot close to the border here, where its deep amethyst-purple tones complement the red clover, *Trifolium rubens*, in the foreground – bereft of its fluffs of crimson flowers at this time of year, but valiantly hanging on to its leaves. Between them, a shock of *Ratibida columnifera* makes a brave final push, attempting to unfurl the last of its blooms before frost arrives. I value these courgeous efforts all the more for their timing – plants reaching beyond their season through sheer tenacity. Behind this grouping, *Miscanthus sinensis* 'Malepartus' waves its feathery farewell, creating a backdrop of movement. While these plants wind down as the growing season concludes, the tawny, purple and silvery tones create a beautiful vignette that catches the low light in ways summer's brighter colours never could.

Ocimum basilicum 'Dark Opal' This beautiful basil is a tender perennial and flowers for a good six months, its blooms addicting pollinators, while the aromatic foliage adds flavour to summer dishes. Reaching up to 75cm (2½ft), it thrives in full sun and well-drained soil with a minimum of maintenance, making it perfect for an attractive, edible pot display. Grown as an annual in cooler climates, it adds height, fragrance and scatterings of leaf for sauces and salads. **HARDINESS: RHS H1C (TYPICALLY GROWN AS AN ANNUAL IN THE UK).**

Trifolium rubens This clump-forming perennial clover hails from the Alps and Pyrenees and is easy to grow from seed in spring. It produces attractive foliage and crimson flower spikes in summer, both of which are perfect for flower arrangements. Reaching around 60cm (2ft) in height, it prefers well-drained soil and a sunny location, and even without flowers, the foliage provides a valuable textural element in autumn. **HARDINESS: RHS H7**

Miscanthus sinensis 'Malepartus' This ornamental grass provides height, movement and late-season interest with its arching foliage and feathery plumes. Reaching heights of 1.5–2m (5–6½ft), it thrives in full sun and well-drained soil. **HARDINESS: RHS H6**

TIPS FOR SUCCESS

- Protect basil from frost by bringing pots indoors during cold snaps; take cuttings to overwinter it, or grow it from seed in spring.
- Deadhead *Trifolium rubens* to encourage fresh new blooms.
- Allow *Ratibida columnifera* to self-seed to maintain a continuous display year after year, or, if you would prefer more control, collect seeds to sow in spring.
- Cut back the *Miscanthus* to ground level in late winter or early spring before new growth emerges.

Golden Echoes

A study in unlikely harmony

Just as late autumn begins, along comes this captivating partnership to catch your eye. The ballet-shoe-pink Japanese anemones pirouette against the golden umbels of fennel, a scene that shouldn't work and yet sings in practice. The foliage of the whitebeam *Sorbus aria* 'Lutescens' provides a near-solid backdrop to these tall perennial performers, its leaves about to begin their buttery autumn transformation.

This combination works because the yellow eyes at the centre of the generously sized, soft pink blooms of *Anemone hupehensis* var. *japonica* pick up the colour of the diaphanous, sulphur umbels of the fennel (*Foeniculum vulgare*). I believe that if nature itself combines the most unlikely of colour pairings, then what's to stop we gardeners doing the same? This duo thrives in well-drained soil in dappled to full sun, offering colour well into autumn when gardens often lack interest. For heavier soils, consider substituting an achillea for the fennel – the anemone will grow almost anywhere!

Anemone hupehensis* var. *japonica This elegant Japanese anemone brings a touch of romance to the late-season garden. The broad yet delicate, cup-shaped flowers, are held on wiry stems, creating a graceful, swaying effect. I always think their seed heads are reminiscent of sea anemones, but that's a whole other story! Reaching around 90cm (3ft) in height, they're happy in most soil conditions, but prefer well-drained, and a spot in partial shade. **HARDINESS: RHS H7**

Foeniculum vulgare An aromatic herb with clouds of foliage that's both beautiful and useful, fennel's feathery leaves provide a soft, textural element, while its flat-topped umbels of tiny yellow flowers attract pollinators. Growing to 1.5–2m (5–6½ft), it thrives in full sun and well-drained soil. **HARDINESS: RHS H5**

***Sorbus aria* 'Lutescens'** This striking whitebeam is a small tree that offers year-round interest. Its green foliage with silver undersides flutters like butterflies when caught in a breeze, providing a beautiful backdrop throughout the summer, before turning a buttery yellow colour in autumn, complementing the colours of any late season display. Reaching up to 8m (26ft), it prefers well-drained soil and a sunny location. **HARDINESS: RHS H6**

> **TIPS FOR SUCCESS**
> - Provide support for *Anemone hupehensis* var. *japonica* in exposed locations to prevent the stems snapping in strong winds.
> - Deadhead the fennel to prevent excessive self-seeding, unless you want more plants in the area.
> - Prune *Sorbus aria* 'Lutescens' in late winter to maintain its shape and remove any dead or damaged branches.
> - Mulch around the base of the plants in spring to help retain soil moisture and suppress weeds.

Woodland Keepsakes

Layered planting to create an autumn glow

Some plants become so woven into our garden's fabric that they would have to come with us if we ever moved house. This autumn scene showcases such treasures – the buttery yellows of *Hamamelis mollis* and *Rhododendron luteum*, both inherited beauties that echo the rays of the summer's sun into autumn's splendour. Between them, I've planted the elegant *Cornus controversa* (the parent species of the wedding cake tree rather than its variegated form) to bridge the gap with its distinctive tiered branches. All are softer than the more emblazoned tones of russet and scarlet that would look misplaced here at the woodland's edge.

This composition flourishes in dappled shade and acid to neutral soil, offering a gorgeous backdrop for garden moments throughout the year. The evergreen foundation of the fern, *Polystichum setiferum* (Divisilobum Group) 'Herrenhausen', provides structural permanence, while the backdrop of mature rhododendrons creates privacy from the lane beyond, which we've crown-lifted so we can still chat with passing neighbours.

Hamamelis mollis The deciduous Chinese witch hazel offers a spectacular display of spidery, fragrant yellow flowers on bare branches from mid-winter to early spring, while in autumn, its rounded leaves turn a glorious soft yellow before falling. Growing slowly to eventually reach 4m (13ft), it prefers moist but well-drained, slightly acidic soil in dappled shade or full sun. **HARDINESS: RHS H5**

Rhododendron luteum Often overlooked for its autumn performance, this deciduous azalea is better known for its spring display of intensely fragrant yellow trumpets. However, its autumn leaves provide an equally spectacular show of oranges and yellows before falling. Growing to 3m (10ft) here, it requires acid soil and protection from cold, drying winds, the woodland edge position suiting it perfectly. **HARDINESS: RHS H6**

Cornus controversa The distinctive, horizontally tiered branches have earned the wedding cake tree its nickname. The species offers elegant structure year-round and is adorned with creamy-white flowers in late spring, followed by small, inky-black berries. Plant it wisely, because even though it grows slowly, it can reach great heights of up to 12m (40ft), and prefers moist, well-drained soil in partial shade. **HARDINESS: RHS H5**

Polystichum setiferum **(Divisilobum Group) 'Herrenhausen'** This evergreen fern is perhaps my favourite of all, providing year-round structure with its elegant, arching, dark green fronds. Creating a lush ground cover, it grows to about 60cm (2ft) tall, and makes a great backdrop for a range of flowering plants in all the colours year-round. Thriving in the dappled shade of deciduous trees and shrubs, it prefers moist, humus-rich soil, yet is remarkably tolerant of dry shade once established. **HARDINESS: RHS H6**

TIPS FOR SUCCESS

- Plant witch hazels where their winter flowers can be appreciated up close, perhaps near a path or seating area.
- Maintain soil acidity for rhododendrons with annual mulches of leaf mould or composted pine needles.
- Allow space for the wedding cake tree to develop its distinctive tiered form without crowding it.
- Crown-lift mature shrubs to create sight lines through them and to improve airflow through the garden.
- In dry periods, prioritise watering newly planted specimens until well-established.

Late Season Lace

Umbels and grasses to catch the autumn light

At this time of year, I embrace the beauty of decline, the transitional charm of plants as their colours fade and they set seed. This combination repeats very well through the borders, pairing the intricate umbels of *Anethum graveolens* 'Mariska' (florist's dill) with the soft-brush plumes of *Pennisetum orientale* 'Flamingo', both set against the indispensable *Eutrochium purpureum*.

When planted in free-draining soil in full sun to light shade, you'll have delicate structure that persists well into autumn's golden days. The feathery textures create a dialogue between the plants, their outline softened by autumn light and enhanced with morning dew or frost. For heavier soils, replace the dill with the more robust *Ligusticopsis wallichiana* (formerly *Selinum wallichianum*), and introduce *Calamagrostis* (instead of *Pennisetum* in exposed sites.

Anethum graveolens 'Mariska' An annual umbellifer, florist's dill provides a constellation of lime-green to golden seed heads atop slender, blue-green stems reaching 1–1.5m (3–5ft) tall. Its feathery foliage adds textural contrast throughout summer, before the flat-topped flower umbels steal the show in autumn. Easy to grow from seed, it's both ornamental and edible – it self-seeds readily, too. **HARDINESS: RHS H4**

Pennisetum orientale 'Flamingo' Transitioning effortlessly from summer into autumn, though late to bloom in the borders, this ornamental grass produces bottlebrush plumes that emerge a bold pink, persisting for weeks before fading to buff in autumn. Growing to 75cm (2½ft), it forms fountains of flower heads that catch the low autumn light beautifully. It prefers well-drained soil and a sunny position, and provides winter interest if left uncut. **HARDINESS: RHS H3**

Eutrochium purpureum This statuesque perennial provides the perfect backdrop, with its robust stems and broad leaves. Its earlier mauve flower clusters may still be providing colour in late autumn, while its strong silhouette anchors the more delicate textures of its companions through the season and into winter, if left standing. **HARDINESS: RHS H7**

TIPS FOR SUCCESS

- Allow dill to self-seed for natural, meadow-like drifts, thinning seedlings where necessary.
- Leave *Pennisetum* standing through winter for structural interest and frost-catching appeal.
- Consider growing dill in groups for greater impact, sowing successionally for an extended display.
- Cut back only when plants begin to collapse in late winter, just before new growth emerges.

Autumn's Last Dance

A bold mix of flowers and foliage for late season texture

At autumn's end, this dynamic combination gives the garden a final burst of energy. The towering *Eutrochium purpureum* stands tall, its faded domed flower clusters softly billowing beside the feathery plumes of *Miscanthus sinensis* 'Malepartus' that shimmer in the low light. The architectural teasel, *Dipsacus laciniatus*, offers textural contrast and will provide structural beauty all winter.

In the background, spires of sky-blue *Salvia uliginosa* in pots rise like wisps of cold breath, accentuating the rich burgundy *Dahlia* 'Chat Noir' and magnificent *Dahlia* 'Labyrinth'. The foliage of a potted olive tree (*Olea europaea*) offers height and winter interest, while glossy *Trachelospermum jasminoides* climbing the shed provides an evergreen backdrop.

This combination accepts a variety of soil conditions, but flourishes in well-drained, fertile soil that retains some moisture. Most plants tolerate clay, if improved with organic matter, creating a display that delights the eye and provides vital late-season forage for pollinators.

TIPS FOR SUCCESS

- Support the tall dahlias with stakes to stop them falling over in strong winds.
- Train *Trachelospermum* horizontally on wires to promote full coverage and plenty of flowers.
- *Miscanthus sinensis* 'Malepartus' is generally pest and trouble free, but dislikes very wet soils.
- Divide *Eutrochium purpureum* every 3–4 years in autumn or spring to maintain its vigour and prevent overcrowding, which can lead to a reduction in blooms.

Salvia uliginosa A robust perennial, reaching up to 2m (6½ft) tall, with lance-shaped leaves and branched, mostly naked stems bearing spikes of sky-blue flowers from late summer to autumn. Ideal for moist but well-drained soils in full sun, I have very successfully grown it in a pot for years, where it adds a cool contrast to warm-toned plants and food for pollinators.
HARDINESS: RHS H4

Dahlia 'Chat Noir' A favourite semi-cactus dahlia of mine, 'Chat Noir' boasts huge flowers, 15–20cm (6–8in) in diameter, with long, narrow petals in a deep, rich red, which glow when backlit. Growing to about 1.2cm (4ft) tall, it provides dramatic colour from midsummer until the first frost and does well in a large pot. Best grown in full sun, lift tubers in winter in colder areas, or mulch heavily. HARDINESS: RHS H3

Olea europaea The Mediterranean olive brings timeless elegance and evergreen structure to this autumn grouping. Its narrow, leathery leaves are grey-green above, with distinctive silvery undersides that shimmer in autumn's softer light. In a large pot, this evergreen shrub or small tree reaches 2–3m (6½ft–10ft), though it can be kept smaller with judicious pruning. It thrives in full sun and needs excellent drainage. In pots, use a gritty, well-draining compost and protect the plant from harsh winter winds. A monthly feed during the growing season keeps it looking its best. HARDINESS: RHS H4, THOUGH BENEFITS FROM WINTER PROTECTION IN COLDER REGIONS

Trachelospermum jasminoides An evergreen climber with glossy leaves and fragrant white flowers in summer. When not in bloom, autumn's touch renders the foliage carmine-ruby, its glossy foliage greening up in spring to deliver year-round interest to trained over structures. Growing to 3-9m (10–29½ft), it thrives in full sun or partial shade with well-drained soil. HARDINESS: RHS H4

Eutrochium purpureum (see p.185)
Miscanthus sinensis **'Malepartus'** (see p.179)
Dipsacus laciniatus (see p.157)
Dahlia **'Labyrinth'** (see p.153)

LATE AUTUMN
WHAT TO DO

Late autumn brings a sense of closure to the garden year, as nature prepares for winter's dormancy. This season is crucial for readying the garden for the cold weather to come and setting the stage for spring's renewal. Key activities include planting tulips, protecting plants likely to succumb to frosts, collecting seed and enriching the soil. The sharp air and occasional frosty mornings provide invigorating conditions for tackling heavier jobs such as border restructuring or creating new planting areas, while you enjoy the low, warm light.

Winterproofing the Garden

As temperatures drop, protecting tender plants becomes essential. Group potted specimens against sheltered walls and move pelargoniums into a greenhouse, conservatory or frost-free porch. For plants that can't be moved, apply a thick layer of mulch around their base. Wrap vulnerable plants such as tree ferns and cannas in horticultural fleece or breathable hessian, securing it carefully to prevent wind damage, while allowing air to circulate. In cold regions, cannas are best lifted and the rhizomes stored inside.

Raise containers on to pot feet to ensure good drainage and prevent waterlogging in winter; this reduces the risk of roots rotting during wet periods and helps to prevent permeable terracotta and clay containers cracking as they freeze then thaw.

Check stakes and tree ties, adjusting any that are too tight to prevent damage to the trunk. Ties that are too loose may need tightening to prevent them rubbing the tree and causing abrasions during winter storms.

This is also the perfect time to clean and store garden furniture, tools and equipment, extending their lifespan and ensuring they're ready for use next spring.

The Great Garden Review

Shorter late autumn days and cosy evenings are perfect times for garden reflection. Brew a warming cup of tea, settle in front of the fire and review those garden photos from the year. It's astonishing what you notice in photographs that you might have missed in the moment.

Try drawing up what I call a 'flower gap analysis' – essentially a timeline of when your garden bloomed and the periods when colour was scarce. This exercise often reveals gaps in the garden's performance, guiding your planning and plant choices for next year. While you're at it, begin browsing seed catalogues and planning next year's additions – there's nothing quite like garden dreaming during autumn evenings.

Leave Foliage to Work its Magic

Here's a thought that might make traditional gardeners wince – leave those leaves where they fall on your borders and listen to the satisfying rustle as you walk past. There's method in this messiness. The foliage will break down over winter, returning nutrients to your soil, while creating hibernation spots for wildlife. The exceptions? Larger leaves from magnolias or rhododendrons, which need chopping up first with your mower, and remove any leaves on your lawn– wet leaves and grass are not happy bedfellows. You can then pile these up in a quiet corner of a border to make a habitat for overwintering garden creatures.

Last-Chance Lawn Care

Only tackle lawn maintenance on a dry day – a wet cut delivers nothing but a shredded, muddy mess. It's prime 'last cut' time when the sun is out, and remember to raise those blades. While you're at it, crisp up the lawn edges – it's remarkable how neat edges keep the whole garden looking smart through winter.

Also give your lawn a thorough going-over by spiking it with the tines of a garden fork. Work some sharp sand mixed with compost into the holes you've made; these channels will help water drain away and feed the soil that's supporting your lawn. This simple task can make all the difference to lawn health throughout the wetter months.

Climate-Conscious Gardening

With our winters becoming wetter, many gardeners are rethinking traditional approaches. Consider creating rain gardens in natural water collection points, installing bog gardens instead of fighting persistent wet spots, and establishing swales to direct water flow. These damp areas offer new and exciting planting opportunities.

Even mulching practices are evolving – while traditional wisdom suggests heavy mulching, there's growing interest in leaving strategic areas of bare soil for beneficial insects such as solitary bees, which use open ground to make their nests, and butterflies that sunbathe in warm, sheltered nooks. Try experimenting by leaving patches of soil exposed near butterfly-friendly plants, creating a thoughtful patchwork that works with nature, not against it.

MY ESSENTIAL DOS AND DON'TS

+ Order bare-root trees, shrubs, and hedging plants, to plant at the end of the season or in winter (see p.217).
+ Prune deciduous trees and shrubs (except *Prunus* species which are pruned in summer) once they're fully dormant.
+ Plant tulips later in the season to reduce the risk of disease.
+ Label lifted dahlias for their winter sleep – late autumn's ritual of tucking treasures safely away until spring calls them back.
+ Clean out bird boxes and put up bird feeders.
+ Create wildlife habitats with log piles and heaps of leaves.
+ Take time to review your garden's performance this year and plan for the next one.

- Walk on sodden lawns – compacted soil creates problems that will persist into next year.
- Be overzealous with tidying – seed heads provide food for birds and winter interest.
- Rush to cut back perennials – their architectural forms add winter structure.
- Disturb hibernating wildlife in quiet corners of the garden.

Lifting and Storing Potted Dahlias for Winter
Protect precious tubers from frost for stunning blooms next year

Winter can be brutal for frost-shy dahlias. After years of gardening, I've perfected a method of lifting and storing their tubers and haven't lost a single plant in years. While timing and technique are crucial, this process will save you money and heartbreak by helping your potted tubers survive until spring.

1 Choose the right time
Llift your dahlias in mid-autumn from pots while they're still in good condition, rather than gambling with a sudden cold snap, as some experts suggest. This also allows you to make way for spring bulbs in the same containers.

2 Cut back the growth
Start by cutting back stems and top growth to about 15cm (6in). This makes lifting them more manageable. Leave one forked stem growing from the top of each tuber – this Y-shaped nub prevents labels from slipping off during winter storage.

3 Lift with care
Work around the edges with a garden knife to free clinging roots from the pot, before removing the entire root ball. Remove compost where possible, using both hands to free the tuber.

4 Clean and inspect
Give each tuber a gentle clean with an old brush to remove excess soil. This process allows you to detect any soft spots or rot, which should be cut away immediately. Keep root trimming to a minimum – just remove the longest roots and any obviously damaged bits. Avoid splitting tubers until spring.

5 Dry thoroughly
Place tubers upside down (stems down, tubers up) for about two weeks. This crucial drying period allows moisture to escape from the hollow stems. Set them in a frost-free, well-ventilated space during this time.

6 Pack for winter sleep
After drying, give tubers one final check. Line storage containers (garden crates or boxes with ventilation holes work well) with newspaper. Add a thin layer of bone-dry peat-free compost, then place the tubers on top, the right way up and spaced apart to prevent rot spreading. Cover them lightly with more dry compost. The ideal storage temperature is 7–13°C (45–55°F) – avoid extremes or fluctuations. An insulated garage or cool cupboard works well. Check your tubers once or twice over winter, removing any that have gone soft or mouldy.

> **Dahlias in Borders Tip:** I leave these planted in the ground, protecting them with a blanket of mulch at least 10cm (4in) deep. This insulating layer helps to shield them from the worst of the winter cold, while allowing me to enjoy the same plants year after year.

Making a Fragrant Paperwhite Display
Create a stunning indoor winter display with delicate, scented blooms

Bringing the garden indoors during the winter months is a wonderful way to enjoy blooms while your garden plants outside are dormant. Paperwhite daffodils, which you can buy now, are perfect for this, transforming from simple bulbs into spectacular blooms right before your eyes, and filling your home with their distinctive fragrance just in time for Christmas.

1 Choose your container
Select a decorative container that suits your style – crystal bowls, vases or vintage containers all work beautifully. Ensure it's deep enough to support your growing stems – about 15cm (6in) is ideal.

2 Create a drainage layer
Add about 5cm (2in) of grit or small stones to the bottom of your container. This crucial layer creates a sump for water and prevents bulb rot. I then add a layer of peat-free compost, to give the bulbs a little extra oomph and to keep my twig supports upright.

3 Position your bulbs
Place your paperwhite bulbs so they're resting on top of your growing medium with their pointed ends facing up and the flat bases slightly nestled into it. Add a touch more grit around the bulbs for stability, leaving the top third exposed. I also add some moss raked from my lawn to give a woodland feel to the display.

4 Add natural supports
Insert birch or hazel twigs around the bulbs before they begin growing. Arrange in a tepee formation, securing loosely with natural twine where they cross at the top. Use more twigs than you think you may need – there are always a few wayward stems that need additional propping up.

5 Water with precision
Use a turkey baster for perfect watering control! This allows you to direct water on to the grit, while keeping the bulbs themselves dry. Only the roots should touch water, never the bulb.

6 Care and maintenance
Turn your pots regularly as they grow to prevent your plants stretching to reach for the light. Keep an eye on water levels (glass vessels are perfect for this), making sure that the bulbs are never submerged. For timing, paperwhites need about 4–5 weeks from planting to flowering. If blooms progress too quickly, move them to a cooler room at around 15°C (59°F); if they're lagging, a warmer position of around 20°C (68°F) can help speed things up.

Early Winter

The landscape transforms in early winter – although this is not a time of absence, as many might assume, but rather a quieter time. Chattering birds have either migrated or become somewhat more selective about their appearances, rustling leaves have fallen, and even the wind seems to move through branches with a more hushed quality. The garden has earned this rest, having worked hard to deliver a technicolour array of hues earlier in the year.

In truth, I find myself oddly energised by the stripped-back borders, the bite of the air after frost, the crunch of fallen leaves on the garden paths. Bundled up as I wander in bold, bright knitwear, beret and mittens, far more colourful than the garden itself, I explore with fresh eyes. I know the garden isn't completely asleep. Below ground it's simply replenishing itself, restoring its energy, ready to produce next year's display.

There's something honest about the garden in early winter. Without the distractions of abundant blooms, the crispness enhances the elegant architecture of bare branches holding strong against the cold and the intricacy of desiccated seed heads inviting you to look closer, to enjoy and admire. On bright, cold mornings when frost transforms the landscape into a crystalline wonderland, I gasp with delight as this apparent dormancy reveals its own kind of magic.

Early winter rewards those who venture outdoors with unexpected discoveries – perhaps the startling crimson berries of holly glistening like jewels, or the surprising fragrance of sweet box (*Sarcococca confusa*) perfuming the air on still days. These are subtle pleasures, certainly, but all the more precious for their rarity. There's a particular quality to early winter light that

Early winter's balancing act – tidying without losing those crucial seed heads that provide structure and food through the cold months ahead

transforms the garden – low, golden and fleeting. It stretches shadows dramatically across lawns and paths, backlights ornamental grasses until they glow like filaments, and illuminates seed heads with an almost reverential precision.

These discoveries inspire my approach to planting schemes. When planning the winter garden, I focus on 'moments of joy' – strategic spots where beauty can be positioned for maximum impact during these darker months. A frost-catching sculptural plant where morning light will hit, a group of containers I can see clearly through the kitchen windows, or a bird feeder hanging from the *Sorbus* tree creating daily moments of connection with the garden, even on the coldest days.

Evergreen shrubs become the backbone of these designs, the garden overseers, watching the bulbs and scatterings of flowers that brave the weather to make use of the few pollinators still around, with little competition. If you have a large garden, I encourage you to arrange these shrubs in rhythmic groups rather than as isolated specimens, creating a sense of intentional structure that appears especially strong when herbaceous plants have retreated.

For winter colour, I advise my clients to rely less on flowers and more on a palette of leaf, bark and berries. A selection might include the flame-coloured stems of *Cornus sanguinea* 'Midwinter Fire', the ghostly white branches of *Rubus thibetanus*, and the peach-streaked creamy bark of *Betula* 'Fascination', all positioned where low winter sunlight will

Time to remove old hellebore foliage – early winter's essential job that reveals emerging blooms and keeps black spot at bay

> *One design technique I particularly recommend for winter gardens is what I call 'borrowed brightness' – positioning plants with winter interest against dark backdrops that make them stand out*

illuminate them from behind. These bright verticals become like living sculptures in the winter garden, drawing the eye in to encourage exploration.

Berries provide vital punctuation marks of colour. As well as the familiar holly and pyracantha, consider the berries of roses (I treasure the hips of the climbing *Rosa* THE SIMPLE LIFE around my front door), hawthorn in a wildlife hedge, and my new favourite, *Callicarpa* PEARL GLAM. This stunning shrub offers violet-purple berries, along with purple foliage that appears early in spring. These fruiting plants serve dual purposes – ornamental value for humans and essential food sources for birds when little else is available.

The approach to winter planting shifts dramatically depending on the garden context. In exposed sites, I prioritise windbreaks of tough evergreens such as *Osmanthus × burkwoodii* that create sheltered microclimates where more delicate winter performers can thrive. Urban gardens benefit from the reflected heat of buildings and paving, allowing marginally tender specimens, including *Grevillea rosmarinifolia* or the winter-flowering *Coronilla valentina* subsp. *glauca* 'Citrina', to flourish against walls that get a lot of direct sun. Woodland gardens also need layers of interest – perhaps an underplanting of snowdrops to flower later in the season beneath the retained leaves of a beech hedge, or rivers of hellebores emboldening areas under deciduous trees as the change of years comes in.

One design technique I particularly recommend for winter gardens is what I call 'borrowed brightness' – positioning plants with winter interest against dark backdrops that make them stand out. A group of silver birch against a yew hedge or vibrant dogwood stems fronting an ivy-covered wall all become more impactful through this simple contrast of light against dark.

Winter containers are crucial mood-lifters when positioned strategically near entrances and viewpoints, where they'll be appreciated every time you step outside. In my own garden, I steer away from structural evergreens as anchors and clipped yew (*Taxus*) balls due to a lack of space. Instead, I prefer to watch and wait for the grit-topped pots of early-flowering bulbs planted in layers for successive waves of interest. The violas and wallflowers (*Erysimum*) will sulk until late winter, but the occasional cheery face of a pansy will burst forth and say good morning, its little blooms appreciated even more due to the lack of competition.

The winter garden requires different maintenance rhythms. While the garden rests, so do I, though I still go out each morning to breathe it all in, to watch the wildlife hop from seed head to dried stem, relishing the meditative quality of these quieter weeks. This time offers a chance to see the garden in repose and appreciate its resilience, safe in the knowledge that it won't be long until flowers return – they do say that half of the joy of gardening is in the anticipation.

By embracing early winter's distinctive qualities, rather than viewing it merely as an absence of summer, we gain a deeper connection to the garden's full cycle. These shortest days offer their own rewards. We discover a quieter garden that sustains us with the smallest of gifts through the darkest days – the spidery blooms of *Hamamelis* arresting you with their scent, and early-flowering snowdrops scattering glints of white against the gloom. These welcome treasures become our companions before the nights close in.

Frost-kissed seed heads catching winter sun, the reward for those who venture out on cold mornings

Winter's Pale Performers

Early snowdrops dancing with architectural ferns

Mixing a range of snowdrop species will give you a remarkably long season of winter interest when there's little else in bloom. Here, *Galanthus woronowii* lights up the shade with its substantial bright green leaves and early flowers, creating a beautiful contrast with the feathery fronds of the soft shield fern, *Polystichum setiferum* (Divisilobum Group) 'Herrenhausen'.

Snowdrops are remarkable plants, containing natural antifreeze proteins that allow them to push through frozen ground and withstand harsh frosts, making early flowering possible. The magic lies in the interplay between their delicate white flowers and bold evergreen textures, enhanced by winter's low light that sometimes creates dramatic shadow patterns. *Galanthus woronowii* blooms from early winter through to midwinter, providing essential colour when the garden feels most barren.

For other early-flowering snowdrops, I recommend *Galanthus plicatus* 'Three Ships' and *Galanthus elwesii* 'Maidwell'. Plant in partial shade with moisture-retentive soil for the best results.

TIPS FOR SUCCESS

- Plant snowdrop bulbs 'in the green', when still in leaf but after the flowers have faded, for the best establishment.
- Choose moisture-retentive but well-drained soil.
- Allow natural leaf litter to accumulate on the soil surface to create a natural mulch and help it to retain moisture.
- Divide snowdrop clumps every 3–4 years after flowering.
- Plant different varieties of snowdrops for a succession of flowers throughout the winter season.

Galanthus woronowii This robust species is among the earliest to flower, its distinctive bright green, strap-like leaves accompanied by nodding white flowers. The substantial foliage provides excellent contrast with finer-textured plants, and it naturalises readily in woodland conditions. Plant in spring in the green (see Tips for success) in partial shade and moisture-retentive soil. **HARDINESS: RHS H5**

***Galanthus plicatus* 'Three Ships'** This variety is often the first in any collection to bloom. The single green markings on the flowers' inner petals create a classic snowdrop appearance. Plant in spring in the green (see tip) in partial shade and moisture-retentive soil; it will quickly form substantial clumps. **HARDINESS: RHS H5**

***Galanthus elwesii* 'Maidwell'** An early-flowering variety with distinctive V-shaped markings on the inner petals. Plant in spring in the green (see Tips for Success) in woodland conditions with moisture-retentive soil. It forms neat clumps of sturdy green foliage, and is perfect for extending the flowering season. **HARDINESS: RHS H5**

***Polystichum setiferum* (Divisilobum Group) 'Herrenhausen'** Beautiful semi-evergreen fern with dark green, filigree fronds and the most spectacular chestnut coloured croziers when j ust about to unfurl. Plant 60cm (2ft) apart in humus-rich, moisture-retentive soil. Prefers partial to full shade. Combines perfectly with early bulbs. **HARDINESS: RHS H5**

Galanthus woronowii brightening up winter **(top left and bottom)**; complemented by *Polystichum setiferum* (Divisilobum Group) 'Herrenhausen' **(top right)**

Winter's Crystals

Structural seed heads adorned with frost's delicate touch

Early winter shares a subtle palette with us that is often overlooked – the warm browns and buffs of structural perennials become the season's colour story, glittering sparkle added by frost's crystalline touch. The light buff of *Miscanthus* plumes, *Phlomis russeliana*'s domed honey-coloured seed heads, and the aster's warm sienna spheres provide indispensable winter interest in my garden, and are transformed into shimmering sculptures after a visit by Jack Frost. The key is to leave the stems standing – this decision rewards you with ongoing visual interest, while providing essential wildlife habitats. Birds feast on the seed heads throughout winter, hollow stems shelter beneficial insects, and the structural framework prevents the garden from feeling empty, especially important in smaller gardens. Underplant these sculptural elements with winter aconites or *Cyclamen coum* as the garden transitions into early spring and the frosts recede.

Miscanthus sinensis **'Malepartus'** This grass delivers warm coppery-brown plumes that create movement in summer and colour in winter. The seed heads bleach to creamy buff as temperatures fall, becoming ethereal when frosted. Essential for winter structure – leave standing until new growth emerges, cutting the foliage back hard to the ground in early spring. Plant in full sun and any reasonable soil. HARDINESS: RHS H6

Dipsacus laciniatus Cut-leaved teasel contributes spiky architectural drama in warm brown tones in winter. This biennial is welcome here for its summer presence, and the early winter geometric seed heads that mature to honey-brown, each crystal-frosted edge creating intricate patterns. The visual interest combined with wildlife value makes it an essential winter performer. Teasel prefers well-drained soil in sun, and because it self-seeds freely, some gardeners worry about it taking over in the garden, but I find it's easy to dig out the offspring that have planted themselves in the wrong place. HARDINESS: RHS H7

Phlomis russeliana At this time of year, Turkish sage offers tiered geometric seed heads in rich buff tones. The whorled heads of this perennial mature to warm biscuit colours, catching frost beautifully to create natural candelabras that provide structural winter interest while supporting wildlife – many insects overwinter in the hollow stems. Plant 45cm (1½ft) apart in spring, in well-drained soil and sun or part shade. Cut old stems to the ground in early spring. HARDINESS: RHS H6

Symphyotrichum **'Vasterival'** This robust aster produces substantial spherical seed heads that age to warm sienna-brown, the stems providing impact in winter. Plant 50cm (1⅔ft) apart in spring in moisture-retentive but well-drained soil and full sun or part shade. Do be aware that this perennial's a runner! Cut back and contain it by pulling out adventurous, wandering roots as new growth emerges. HARDINESS: RHS H7

Symphyotrichum 'Vasterival' **(opposite)**

TIPS FOR SUCCESS

- Leave all seed heads standing from autumn for colour and wildlife.
- Position in full sun for richest colour development.
- Water well during first year, after which these plants are all drought-tolerant.
- Cut back the stems of seed heads in early spring as new growth appears.
- Allow natural seeding for a continuous display year after year.
- Group the perennials and teasels in odd numbers (3–7) for maximum impact.

Phlomis russeliana

Miscanthus sinensis 'Malepartus' and *Dipsacus laciniatus*

Opposite *Miscanthus sinensis* 'Malepartus' and *Dipsacus laciniatus*

Above *Phlomis russeliana*

Frosted Textures

Bold leaves to brighten the winter garden

Frost brings the winter garden to life when it visits, transforming everyday evergreen ground cover into something altogether more theatrical. Unlike my structural seed head combinations, this one is all about foliage – from *Epimedium*'s heart-shaped leaves edged in crystal, to soft shield ferns, *Polystichum setiferum* (Divisilobum Group) 'Herrenhausen', looking like they've been dipped in icing sugar, every leaf margin is highlighted with diamond dust, emphasising the colour, tone and texture.

I use a mulch of fine composted bark mulch and leaf mould collected from my garden, leaving it to decompose into the borders over time, where it adds nutrients and blends into the woodland setting.

Just out of shot the flowers of a *Helleborus argutifolius*, heavy with the frost, bow their heads, but will bounce fully upright again once the day warms up. These frosted plants complement the stems of seed heads and are equally rewarding for winter interest.

TIPS FOR SUCCESS

- Plant in autumn for best establishment before winter.
- Match plants to their preferred light conditions in a border.
- Allow sufficient space for *Epimedium*, which is a vigorous spreader.
- Cut back most of the old *Epimedium* foliage in late winter to enjoy the flowers.
- Position plants near the house to appreciate the evergreen cover and frosted spectacle from your windows.

Epimedium × *versicolor* **'Sulphureum'**
An evergreen perennial growing to about 35cm (1ft), it forms clumps of red-tinted, light green leaves that create reliable ground cover for shaded areas. Primrose-yellow flowers, 2cm (¾in) wide, appear in early spring above the foliage, just as the new growth emerges, providing additional interest. Plant in partial shade and moist, well-drained soil. Cut back old foliage in late winter to showcase the emerging flowers and new growth. **HARDINESS: RHS H7**

Sedum takesimense **ATLANTIS** RHS Chelsea Plant of the Year 2019, this little sedum forms neat rosettes of variegated, scalloped leaves that spread to create a layer of leafy ground cover. Chartreuse flowers, attractive to bees, appear from midsummer. Plant in full sun to partial shade and well-drained soil; it's very drought-tolerant once established. This sedum also works well in containers or as border edging. **HARDINESS: RHS H7**

Helleborus argutifolius The Corsican hellebore's bold, three-lobed leaves provide robust winter structure. Plants reach 60–90cm (2–3ft) in height, and produce long-lasting clusters of pale green flowers for many weeks from late winter. This architectural perennial tolerates drier conditions than most hellebores, and thrives in partial shade and well-drained soil. Cut back the spent flowering stems at the base after blooming ends (they look wonderful in a vase), to make room for new, emerging shoots. **HARDINESS: RHS H5**

Polystichum setiferum **(Divisilobum Group) 'Herrenhausen'** (see p. 204)

Beauty in Decay

A symphony of brown seed heads and stems

I've always appreciated every stage of a plant's life cycle, including its graceful decline. These early-winter images capture that bittersweet moment when plants complete their circle, returning to the soil from which they emerged. The warm browns and golds of withered seed heads, the skeletal beauty of spent flower structures, and the rich textures of fading foliage create their own compelling colour story. *Phlomis*, with its candelabra-like seed heads; the delicate spikelets of *Calamagrostis* brushing against *Crocosmia*'s faded, leather-like leaves, with their distinctive markings; gladioli's distinctive pods; and *Betonica*'s neat brushes all add to this winter tapestry. Their decay becomes fertile ground for wildlife – seed eaters find nourishment, while countless creatures discover winter refuge. There's something deeply satisfying about witnessing this natural transformation, rather than rushing to tidy it away. These moments remind us that endings are simply beginnings wearing different clothes.

Calamagrostis brachytricha By early winter, the Korean feather reed grass, with its delicate, fluffy seed heads in warm buff tones, creates soft, hazy effects as it brushes beautifully against other plants. **HARDINESS: RHS H6**

Crocosmia × crocosmiiflora **'George Davison'** A soft yellow-flowered crocosmia whose sword-like leaves fade to warm khaki tones. After summer flowering, the rigid vertical foliage develops character through winter, its leather-like texture creating a striking contrast with softer plants and framing fluffy grass seed heads brilliantly. Plant in well-drained soil in part shade, and cut back stems in late winter/early spring. **HARDINESS: RHS H5**

Gladiolus **'Velvet Eyes'** After the summer blooms have faded, distinctive three-valved seed pods develop on the tall stems of this beautiful gladiolus. The pods split to reveal glossy black seeds, creating architectural winter interest both in the garden and in arrangements for the home. Plant corms in spring, 10cm (4in) deep and 15cm (6in) apart; lift them in winter in cold areas or mulch heavily. **HARDINESS: RHS H3–H4**

Betonica officinalis **'Hummelo'** Betony forms tidy clumps of upright stems, with neat, cylindrical, brush-like seed heads that mature to rich brown in early winter, above basal semi-evergreen leaves. Excellent for winter structure and wild bird food, plant it in well-drained soil and full sun or partial shade; cut it back in early spring. **HARDINESS: RHS H7**

Phlomis russeliana (see p. 207)

> ### TIPS FOR SUCCESS
> - Resist autumn tidying – winter structures deserve appreciation.
> - Leave seed heads standing until spring growth appears.
> - Position near windows for winter viewing pleasure.
> - Create dedicated 'decay' areas to benefit wildlife.
> - Cut back only what's truly unsightly or diseased in early winter.
> - Use winter browns as part of your colour palette.
> - Collect seeds from some plants to to sow in spring.

Phlomis russeliana **(top left)**; *Calamagrostis brachytricha* and *Crocosmia × crocosmiiflora* 'George Davison' **(top right)**; *Gladiolus* 'Velvet Eyes' **(bottom left)**; *Betonica officinalis* 'Hummelo' **(bottom right)**

EARLY WINTER
WHAT TO DO

Early winter signals the garden's transition to slower rhythms. It's a time to consolidate rather than create, as growth effectively stops and the garden settles into dormancy, shifting our focus from active cultivation to preservation and forward planning. The garden is now resting and we become custodians, ensuring that the structures remain sound, protection is adequate, and our preparations set the stage for a successful growing season ahead. Early winter's tasks are subtle but crucial – small actions that safeguard months of hard work, while creating opportunities for next year's displays.

Protect Tender Container Plants

Move frost-sensitive potted plants to sheltered spots before winter really bites, and wrap larger containers in bubble plastic or hessian sacking – it's like giving your plants winter jackets. Group smaller pots together where they'll benefit from shared warmth. Always lift containers up on pot feet, timber offcuts or bricks if they are standing on hard surfaces to prevent waterlogging, taking care that these props don't cover drainage holes on the undersides of your pots.

Winterproof your Plants

As the weather grows colder, focus on protecting what's already established rather than planting new. Apply mulch around shrubs planted in recent years – they need the extra insulation while settling in. Check tree ties and loosen them if necessary as trunks expand, and ensure climbing plants are properly secured before winter winds arrive.

Mend your Garden's Structures

Early winter offers the ideal time for structural maintenance while plants are dormant. Check fences, gates and supports for loose bolts or rotting timber – better to fix things now than discover damage after winter storms or when plants are actively growing in spring. Also clear gutters on sheds and greenhouses to prevent ice damage. A drop of oil on door hinges prevents them seizing in cold weather.

Prepare for Winter Weather

Reduce the sail on evergreen shrubs by lightly pruning them to prevent wind damage. Clear leaves from paths to make sure they don't become slippery and from lawns where they could damage the turf, adding the collected foliage directly to the borders as a mulch. Store garden furniture and ornaments that might suffer in rough weather, and check your greenhouse panes – loose glass panels can become seriously dangerous.

Support Garden Wildlife

Natural food sources become scarce in early winter, so keep your bird feeders topped up (clean them regularly to stop the spread of disease) and provide fresh water regularly. Create shelter areas for wildlife with piles of pruned material. Compost heaps provide valuable overwintering habitat for beneficial insects – keep them accessible but partly cover the top (I use a bit of old carpet) to protect the upper layers from frost.

Plant Bare-Root and Root-Balled Trees

Early winter is prime time for planting bare-root and root-balled trees – these dormant plants are cheaper than container-grown specimens and often establish better. Bare-root trees arrive with their exposed roots wrapped in damp material, while root-balled plants come with soil around their roots, wrapped in hessian or wire mesh. Both need planting immediately upon arrival. Soak bare roots for a few hours before planting. You will not need to soak root-balled trees, and don't remove the hessian or wire cages before planting, as both will rot away naturally once in the ground. The dormant season gives roots time to establish before spring growth begins, creating stronger, more resilient trees.

MY ESSENTIAL DOS AND DON'TS

+ Clear paths of fallen leaves for safe winter access.
+ Group container plants in sheltered areas to protect them from frost.
+ Check stored dahlia tubers every month for signs of rot.
+ Maintain bird feeding stations through winter.
+ Secure climbing plants against winter winds.
+ Service tools before winter storage.
+ Plant bare-root roses and deciduous shrubs while dormant.
+ Prune apple and pear trees to maintain shape and encourage fruiting.
+ Position new bird boxes ready for spring.
+ Mulch newly planted shrubs for frost protection.
+ Insulate outdoor taps and pipework to prevent freezing.
+ Clean greenhouse glass to maximise winter light levels reaching the plants inside.

- Dig heavy soil in wet conditions as this damages its structure.
- Undertake major pruning of deciduous or evergreen plants.
- Walk on frozen lawns which damages grass structure.
- Store damp tools which promotes rust, or even worse, leave them outside!

Early Winter Sweet Pea Sowing
Start now for a garden filled with summer scent

Experienced gardeners know early winter is the ideal time to sow sweet peas. Starting these scented climbers now creates robust plants by spring, ready to be planted out for stunning summer displays. This simple table-top project requires minimal equipment while maximising flowering potential in the months ahead.

1 Prepare your equipment
Set up root trainers or recycled toilet rolls in a standard seed tray. Fill the containers with good quality, peat-free multi-purpose compost, leaving a space of about 2.5cm (1in) at the top. Gather seed packets, plant labels, and a fine-rosed watering can.

2 Sow seeds
Press one seed into the compost surface of each module or toilet roll, then cover with 1cm (½in) of fresh compost. I never bother to pre-soak the seed and haven't ever had a problem, despite books telling you this is what you should do – perhaps the sweet pea seeds don't read them. Label each variety immediately with the name and date – remembering which is which becomes impossible later. Water gently until the compost resembles a well-wrung sponge, not a puddle.

3 Create good growing conditions
Position seed trays in a bright spot away from direct radiator heat. Germination typically occurs within 7–10 days: check morning and evening for emerging shoots.

4 Transition outdoors
When seedlings develop four pairs of true leaves, gradually acclimatise them to outdoor temperatures. Move them to a cold frame, unheated greenhouse or a clear-lidded storage box with drainage holes, to provide some overnight protection while exposing them to daylight. I promise you they're much hardier than you think – mine have been outside with protection in snow.

5 Overwinter successfully
Maintain barely moist conditions – sweet peas detest waterlogged roots. These hardy climbers benefit from cool winter conditions, developing stronger root systems and sturdier growth in response to the lower outdoor temperatures.

6 Prepare for final planting
Well-established plants with robust root systems will be ready for garden planting as soon as they're substantial plants – they're frost hardy, so you won't have to wait. Plant them out into the borders, incorporating plenty of home-made compost or well-rotted manure when you do to support these hungry plants.

Garden Tool Care
Service your equipment, ready for next year's tasks

Early winter is the perfect season for essential tool maintenance, since there's less to do in the garden. Investing time now in cleaning, sharpening and storing equipment properly will extend your tools' lifespans and make sure they're ready to perform when you leap into action come spring. I choose a sunny day, turn on the radio and get ready to show my faithful tools some love.

1 Collect and clean systematically
Gather all cutting implements – secateurs, hori hori knives, pruning saws and loppers. Scrub each one thoroughly with hot soapy water and a stiff brush, ensuring soil deposits are removed from hinges, serrated edges, and all mechanisms. Rinse completely and dry thoroughly.

2 Sharpen precisely
Using a quality tool sharpener (ceramic or diamond-based), work along each blade's bevelled edge in consistent, single-direction strokes. For delicate instruments like your hori hori, employ gentle pressure.

3 Protect and lubricate
Apply a thin coat of appropriate oil (WD-40 or 3-in-1) to all metal components, working the product into pivot points and spring mechanisms. This crucial step prevents rust formation and keeps them operating smoothly. Remove excess oil with a clean cloth, and they're ready to go.

4 Service digging equipment
Clean larger tools – spades, forks, shovels, rakes and hoes – removing stubborn clods of soil from their tines and blades. Apply linseed oil to wooden handles to prevent weather damage and splitting. Inspect connections between handles and blades, tightening screws, where necessary, if yours have them.

5 Organise your storage
Return specialised tools to appropriate holsters (secateurs, knives, saws) to keep them safe and their blades sharp and protected. I confess mine live in a large vase by my kitchen sink; I'm sure you'll have your own quick-to-reach place for yours. Store larger tools in a dry location, preferably hung from hooks, so they are easier to reach and won't get bent out of shape. If you've space, you could think about making a maintenance station with a sand and oil mix in a bucket for easy cleaning throughout the season.

Late Winter

The scent of soil warming under strengthening sun – earthy, mineral, alive – is often my first clue that late winter has arrived. The garden hovers in that in-between state – not quite released from winter's grip, but definitely stirring with new life. The light stretches a bit longer each day, and though the garden might still look dormant to casual observers, those who look closely will spot the first signs of awakening: swelling buds on bare branches, the determined spears of early bulbs pushing through cold soil, and the gradually intensifying chorus of birdsong that announces nature's reawakening.

I've always treasured this transitional season for its promise and anticipation. There's something genuinely hopeful about witnessing these first stirrings, small but resolute assertions of life's persistence. I find myself wandering the garden with secateurs in hand, trimming a bit here and there, but really I'm hunting for changes – hellebore buds showing colour, the silvery catkins of *Garrya elliptica* as they lengthen, the first green tips of bulbs appearing in unexpected places. Each discovery feels like a small victory, a confirmation that the garden's pulse is quickening after winter's slower rhythms.

When designing for late winter interest, I focus on plants that bridge the gap between winter's austerity and spring's abundance. My palette now celebrates the subtle, not least because that's what the season's plants deliver – ivory whites, pale yellows and the softest pinks and purples – colours that may seem slightly underwhelming in summer's brighter light, but appear luminous against winter's muted backdrop. These gentle tones capture and reflect the strengthening late season sunshine, bringing light into the garden when it's most appreciated.

First stirrings – iris breaking through, watering cans ready for action – this is when anticipation reaches fever pitch

As we complete our journey through the garden's year of colour, late winter offers perhaps the most valuable lesson of all – that colour need not be abundant to be meaningful. The carefully placed blue of a single *Iris reticulata* against dark mulch can be more impactful than a hundred summer blooms competing for attention. The emerging colour in late winter gardens is like a whispered secret rather than a shout – *Pieris*, with its chains of pink buds hanging like tiny lanterns; the surprising salmon-orange stems of the coral bark dogwood, (*Salix alba* var. *vitellina* 'Britzensis') catching low sunlight; or the butter-yellow starburst of *Hamamelis* against a clear blue sky. I've found that photographing the garden now reveals colours invisible to the casual glance – the burgundy flush on emerging peony shoots, the russet edges of unfurling fern fronds, the jade green of moss revived by winter rain. These are colours that reward the observant gardener, creating a quieter but no less gratifying chromatic experience than the obvious flamboyance of high summer hues.

The nodding bells of hellebore hybrids have become must-haves in my late winter garden, their flowers in shades ranging from purest white through pink to deepest plum providing weeks of reliable colour. Unlike the spring bulbs that are here and gone in a flash, these sturdy perennials persist for months, their downward-facing blossoms perfectly designed to protect pollen from winter rain and snow.

For early colour beyond the usual suspects, I'm particularly drawn to *Cyclamen coum*, whose marbled leaves and bright pink flowers appear from mid-winter onwards. Each variety has its own character – the way the stems hold their flowers, the distinct patterns on the leaves, the subtle variations in their pink tones.

> *As we complete our journey through the garden's year of colour, late winter offers perhaps the most valuable lesson of all – that colour need not be abundant to be meaningful*

Late winter tendrils of *Trachelospermum jasminoides* flushed with coral – proof that my hardest-working climber never truly rests

Scent becomes even more noticeable in the late winter garden, often alerting me to something in flower before I've spotted it, which is why in my garden I've planted a late winter corner featuring plants that specifically offer perfume during this challenging season. After recommending it to clients for years, I finally treated myself to a *Daphne bholua* 'Jacqueline Postill', positioning it where its scented clusters of purplish-pink and white flowers greet me on grey mornings. I've underplanted it with simple ferns, rather than anything too fussy, which might compete with it.

If I had the space for it, a *Viburnum* × *bodnantense* 'Dawn' would reside there, too. Earning its place in larger gardens, its richly fragrant pink flowers on bare branches appear when little else dares to bloom. These aren't just pretty but serve a vital ecological function, providing early nectar for the first emerging pollinators of the season, with the scent guiding them to the precious supplies.

Vertical interest becomes particularly important now, when much of the garden remains at ground level. The elegant catkins of the corkscrew hazel (*Corylus avellana* 'Contorta') dangle like peculiar ornaments from twisted branches, creating living sculptures against the sky. The pink-tinged buds of the winter-flowering cherry (*Prunus* × *subhirtella* 'Autumnalis Rosea') open gradually from the start of the new year onwards, producing delicate blossoms that appear almost miraculous against winter's starkness. I've always had a soft spot for *Clematis cirrhosa* var. *purpurascens* 'Freckles', too, with its pale cream, nodding, bell-shaped flowers, heavily freckled inside with rusty maroon. This wonderfully vigorous winter-flowering climber was one of the first plants I learned about at horticultural college, and I really must find a spot for it this year.

As the garden begins its gradual reawakening, I want to reach out and touch every bit I see. I find myself noticing the tactile quality of emerging growth – the felted backs of unfurling magnolia buds, the smooth glossiness of hellebore leaves, the papery sheaths protecting nascent bulb flowers. These textural elements reward close inspection and add another dimension to the late winter garden experience.

This time of year teaches us the value of patience and attention. It reminds us that transformation rarely happens overnight, but through a series of incremental changes that build toward something wonderful. By embracing this season, we can find genuine pleasure in winter's final weeks, discovering beauty in the subtle signs of revival, and taking quiet satisfaction in knowing that spring's abundance, though still mostly hidden, is already unfolding beneath the surface. The garden is warming up for its annual performance – beginning not with a fanfare, but with gentle whispers that reward those who take the time to listen.

Iris reticulata 'Angela' brings the first bolt soft blue – everything we've been waiting for through winter's long months and the promise of what's to come

Tough Miniatures

Late winter bulbs sparkling in terracotta pots

It's uplifting to look out of the window in the depths of late winter and see terracotta pots brimming with colour when frost still clings to the pane. These pots will continue to flower for months and the secret lies in layering (see p.166). Right now, *Iris reticulata* varieties provide impact with their jewel-like blooms, while crocuses emerge to extend the display as the irises fade, with plenty more to come, too. The blue-and-purple palette works because it creates depth and a cold-defying elegance that makes me wonder at the power of plants, all without overwhelming the eye. Warmth is provided by the orange crocuses at their feet offering a counterpoint and valuable food source for early-season pollinators. For added interest, use winter-flowering pot toppers such as violas and wallflowers (*Erysimum cheiri*) as I have, which though resting now in the cold of the season, will burst back into bloom once temperatures rise. Narcissi are planted for later interest, too. Pots can be turned, moved and rearranged to keep the display, and your view from inside, interesting.

TIPS FOR SUCCESS

- Plant bulbs in layers: irises 10cm (4in) deep and crocuses 7–8cm (3–3½in), with 5cm (2in) gaps between species.
- Add a 3:1 mix of standard peat-free multi-purpose potting compost and horticultural grit for increased drainage.
- Water sparingly during active growth, avoiding waterlogged conditions.
- Deadhead regularly to prolong flowering and prevent seed formation.
- Allow foliage of both irises and crocuses to die back naturally and feed the bulbs, which will help to boost next season's performance.

Iris **'Pauline'** **(Reticulata)** This early purple beauty delivers rich colour when gardens are at their bleakest. Compact at just 15cm (6in) tall, 'Pauline' works beautifully in containers, and the flowers typically last two or three weeks, coping with frost where taller blooms may falter. Plant bulbs 10cm (4in) deep in autumn, ensuring excellent drainage by adding horticultural grit to the compost (see Tips for Success). HARDINESS: RHS H6

Iris **'Blue Note'** **(Reticulata)** A reliable companion to 'Pauline', offering slightly lighter purple-blue tones, its fragrance is an added bonus on milder winter days. It has the same planting needs as 'Pauline' and will also return year after year; group several corms together for impact, as individual blooms are small but collectively create plenty of colour. HARDINESS: RHS H6

Crocus olivieri subsp. *balansae* **'Orange Monarch'** Following the irises, these cheerful orange goblets emerge to keep the colour going. The warm tones provide essential contrast to the cool blue scheme, while the crocus's grass-like foliage disappears tidily after flowering. Plant corms 7–8cm (3–3½in) deep in between the iris bulbs in the top layer of your lasagne (see p.166). Replant them in borders when the pots have finished blooming. HARDINESS: RHS H6

Mixed varieties of winter-flowering *Viola* These workhorses keep flowering through all but the coldest spells. Favourite winter-flowering varieties include 'Tiger Eye Red', 'Sorbet XP Morpho' and 'Sorbet Honeybee'. They are surprisingly resilient in sheltered spots, not blooming when temperatures plummet but flowering again when the weather warms up. Replace annually for best results. HARDINESS: RHS H4–H5

Mixed varieties of *Erysimum* Only just showing here, these wallflowers provide foliage cover and will bloom later in spring to provide colour and perfume until it's time to replant my pots with dahlia tubers. All are wonderful in supporting early pollinators when little else is in bloom. HARDINESS: RHS H5

Eranthis hyemalis, *Crocus olivieri* subsp. *balansae* 'Orange Monarch' and *Iris* 'Pauline' (Reticulata')

Crocus olivieri subsp. *balansae* 'Orange Monarch'

Opposite *Iris* 'Pauline' (Reticulata)

Above Frosted but unbothered – these tough little bulbs are late winter's true heroes

White Winter Elegance

Snowdrops to treasure as the seasons turn

When most gardens are sleeping, few sights capture late winter's quiet beauty quite like this classic trio. The combination brings light and elegance to sheltered corners and shady spots, creating a delicate display that speaks volumes without shouting. The pristine droplets of *Galanthus* 'Magnet' hang like tiny chandeliers among the feathery, evergreen fronds of *Polystichum setiferum* (Divisilobum Group) 'Herrenhausen', perhaps the most useful fern in my planting arsenal, bringing year-round structure to challenging spots. In the background, hellebore blooms provide gentle warmth and vintage charm. This scheme isn't just planted for aesthetics – it's practical gardening that works with my soil and conditions. Each plant thrives in partial shade and moisture-retentive soil with minimal fuss. Plant this combination once, and it will return year after year, becoming more established and confident with each season, and requiring virtually no maintenance beyond an annual mulch of leaf mould.

Galanthus **'Magnet'** This wonderful snowdrop typically flowers in late winter, though exact flowering times vary from year to year, influenced by local weather conditions and the region's climate. In warmer areas, it can bloom earlier in late winter, while colder regions may see slightly delayed blooms. Named for its distinctive long, strong pedicels (flower stalks) that seem to thrust their blooms upwards, drawing the eye to them like magnets. The graceful, pendulous white flowers, with their characteristic bright green markings, dance in winter breezes, creating movement in otherwise still landscapes. **HARDINESS: RHS H5**

Polystichum setiferum **(Divisilobum Group) 'Herrenhausen'** Perhaps the most useful fern in my planting arsenal, this compact soft shield fern brings year-round structure to challenging spots. Its densely textured fronds keep their colour through winter, and it thrives in dry shade, too – a notoriously difficult combination. Perfect ground cover beneath trees where grass struggles, it provides valuable texture throughout the seasons, while its manageable size makes it ideal for smaller gardens. Cut back old fronds in spring to reveal fresh growth. **HARDINESS: RHS H7**

Hellebore (garden variety) This particular hellebore, sourced from my RHS Hampton Court show garden many years ago, holds sentimental value alongside horticultural merit, although I've lost the label. Its nodding blooms in soft, speckled tones add gentle warmth to winter's palette. For similar effects, consider *Helleborus* × *lemperii* HGC 'Liara', *Helleborus niger* Harvington hybrids, or the sophisticated colours of the Helleborus Gold Collection, including MARLON, the Ice N' Roses series such as MERLOT, and VICTORIA, which is one of the ViV series. On my wish list remains *Helleborus* × *hybridus* 'Yellow Lady' – a variety I'm particularly keen to add to my collection. Plant in humus-rich, well-drained soil and resist moving once established. **HARDINESS: RHS H5–7**

TIPS FOR SUCCESS

- Plant snowdrops 'in the green' (see p.204) between late winter and mid-spring for best establishment.
- Mulch annually with leaf mould to replicate natural woodland conditions.
- Allow snowdrop foliage to die back naturally – resist the urge to tidy too early.
- Cut back fern fronds in late winter to reveal the emerging spring growth.
- Position in dappled shade with shelter from harsh winds.
- Water during establishment but once settled, this combination is remarkably drought-tolerant.

Crocus Crescendo

Tiny bulbs that create a captivating winter carnival

When the calendar promises spring, but winter still lingers, these early bulbs create impact entirely out of proportion to their size. This is what I call my 'early bird' combination, designed to deliver colour when most gardens are still bare. Easily achieved through layered planting (see p.166), the purple *Crocus* 'Ruby Giant' provides the main focus, while the golden winter aconite (*Eranthis hyemalis* Cilicica Group) adds sunny punctuation marks. The 'Orange Monarch' crocus joins later, and the grape hyacinth *Muscari latifolium* will offer its distinctive two-tone spikes once the crocus fades.

The purple-orange-yellow palette creates harmony as the colours appear naturally in sequence, the combination flowering for 6–8 weeks, from late winter through early spring. An underplanting of several varieties of narcissi will be joining the parade next. Plant in full sun or dappled shade – containers work brilliantly, allowing you to reposition them for maximum impact.

Crocus 'Ruby Giant' Of all the *Crocus tommasinianus* varieties, 'Ruby Giant' wins for sheer presence – the flowers are nearly twice the size of species crocuses, yet retain their naturalistic charm. Deep purple goblets open wide on sunny days to reveal silvery interiors with golden stamens. Perfect for naturalising in lawns, too, where it multiplies happily without becoming invasive. Plant corms 7–8cm (3–3½in) deep in autumn. **HARDINESS: RHS H6**

***Eranthis hyemalis* Cilicica Group** These golden winter buttercups bring sunshine when we need it most. More refined than the common winter aconite, with bronze-tinged foliage beneath glossy yellow cups, the flowers offer up essential early nectar for pollinators. This little plant works well in both containers and borders. Plant tubers 5cm (2in) deep in pots or the ground in autumn – it can be slow to establish in a border but will eventually form self-seeding colonies. **HARDINESS: RHS H5**

Muscari latifolium The aristocrat of grape hyacinths, currently showing emerging foliage here. Elegant two-toned flower spikes – deep purple lower bells crowned with lighter blue, push out of broad, ribbed leaves that provide structural contrast to the delicate blooms. It shows admirable restraint, rarely self-seeding to nuisance levels, while maintaining a reliable annual performance. Plant bulbs 10cm (4in) deep in autumn. **HARDINESS: RHS H5**

***Crocus olivieri* subsp. *balansae* 'Orange Monarch'** (see p.231)

> **TIPS FOR SUCCESS**
>
> - Layer bulbs by depth: *Muscari* 10cm (4in), crocus 7–8cm (3–3½in), *Eranthis* 5cm (2in) deep.
> - Plant bulbs on a layer of grit to improve drainage if growing in a border with heavy soil such as clay.
> - Plant in sun or dappled shade – avoid deep shade for the best flowering.
> - Allow all foliage to die back naturally to feed next year's display.
> - If you're keeping this combination in containers, refresh the top layer of compost annually in autumn but avoid disturbing established bulbs.
> - In borders, plant bulbs in drifts rather than in regimented rows for a natural effect.
> - Water sparingly – these bulbs prefer drier conditions once established.

Purple Crocus 'Ruby Giant' and yellow Eranthis hyemalis Cilicica Group; Muscari latifolium emerging **(top right)**; *Crocus olivieri subsp. balansae 'Orange Monarch' adds a rich orange to the whole display* **(bottom)**

Pretty Petticoats

The earliest narcissus to brighten winter pots

I prefer to plant bulbs that deliver small but beautiful blooms in pots, bringing them up to eye level, where their intricate details become the stars of the show, particularly in winter. This is precisely why I prefer the hoop petticoat daffodil, *Narcissus bulbocodium* 'Arctic Bells', elevated in containers rather than in ground-level plantings – its distinctive flared petals resemble Victorian hoop petticoats, hence the name. These diminutive daffodils flower for weeks, creating a long-lasting display. Here, they're paired with emerging *N.* 'Tête-à-tête' and orange *Crocus olivieri* subsp. *balansae* 'Orange Monarch'– a combination that extends the flowering season beautifully. What makes this work is the varied flower forms: flared vases, cups and goblets creating textural interest, while maintaining a harmonious colour palette. Plant the bulbs in autumn in pots of well-drained compost and position in full sun on patios, tables or raised planters.

Narcissus bulbocodium **'Arctic Bells'**
These distinctive daffodils deserve prime positions, where their unique butter-yellow hoop-skirted flowers can be appreciated up close. 'Arctic Bells' offers excellent garden performance, flowering for weeks rather than days like many daffodils. The pale-yellow petals flare dramatically around tiny trumpets, creating an almost architectural silhouette. Perfect in containers where overhead viewing reveals their true beauty. Plant bulbs 10–12cm (4–5in) deep in autumn, the flowers return reliably year after year, especially if planted in raised beds. **HARDINESS: RHS H6**

Narcissus **'Tête-à-tête'** Just breaking through the gravel here, this reliable miniature will soon add its perky yellow faces to the display. At just 15cm (6in) tall, it's perfectly proportioned for containers, and packs impressive flower power – often producing two blooms per stem. The golden-yellow cups and reflexed petals deliver classic daffodil charm in miniature. Plant bulbs 10cm (4in) deep alongside other varieties. It multiplies freely year after year, creating better displays as time goes on. **HARDINESS: RHS H6**

Crocus olivieri subsp. *balansae* **'Orange Monarch'** (see p.231)

TIPS FOR SUCCESS

- Use containers with excellent drainage, mixing grit with peat-free multipurpose compost – bulbs hate waterlogged conditions.
- Plant narcissus 10–12cm (4–5in) deep, crocus 7–8cm (3–3½in), with 5cm (2in) spacing between varieties.
- Position containers where morning sun hits but afternoon shade prevents the flowers overheating.
- Water moderately during growth, reduce after flowering.
- Deadhead spent flowers but allow foliage to yellow and die back naturally.
- Feed with slow-release bulb fertiliser in autumn to bolster next year's display.
- Refresh the grit/gravel mulch annually to keep the display looking smart.

LATE WINTER
WHAT TO DO

Late winter's transitional energy invites gentle action before spring's rush begins, and if I'm wrapped up well, frankly I always consider time outdoors as time well spent. With little gardening to be done, as the light strengthens and the soil slowly warms, there is time to ponder the garden. Think about how to best make use of your outdoor space, so that it will provide months of glorious colour for you to enjoy, not only in the coming season, but this time next year, too. Take your camera and notebook outside, then settle indoors in front of a fire to make your lists and plan for future displays.

Maintaining Colourful Stems for Winter Interest

Late winter is the perfect time to rejuvenate dogwoods (*Cornus*) and willows (*Salix*) that produce colourful stems, ensuring next year's vibrant display. Cut back one-third of the oldest stems to 10cm (4in) from the ground – this encourages fresh, brightly coloured new growth that will provide a stunning display next winter. Leave the youngest stems (those that have the most vivid colour) untouched. Work on an annual rotation, pruning different sections each year to maintain some height, while ensuring continuous renewal. This technique works brilliantly for red-stemmed *Cornus alba* 'Sibirica', yellow-stemmed *C. sericea* 'Flaviramea' and coloured willows such as *Salix alba* var. *vitellina*.

Strategic Late Winter Pruning

Late winter pruning shapes both structure and future colour. Trim winter-flowering shrubs such as witch hazel (*Hamamelis*) and viburnum after their displays fade, removing dead or crossing branches. Tentatively cut back ornamental grasses and the old stems of sedums and echinaceas that have fallen over or look untidy, giving the garden a more considered look, rather than unkempt disarray, but leave the major cut back until early spring when temperatures have risen, allowing garden wildlife to continue its winter hibernation.

Propagation and Division Opportunities

Late winter offers a unique propagation window. Divide snowdrops 'in the green' immediately after flowering – this is the best time for establishing bigger drifts next year. Take evergreen cuttings from *Sarcococca* and *Viburnum tinus* for future plantings while these shrubs are dormant.

Tempting though it is to start sowing hardy annuals indoors, apart from sweet peas, I sit on my hands, as seed sown now needs extra attention, grow lights and care. I prefer to wait until early spring, and find that annuals sown then soon catch up, given the higher light levels. That said, it's a great time to organise, clean and prepare your propagation equipment before the rush: check the seed dates on your packets for viability, order varieties you don't have and would like to grow, and think about your combinations, organising your seeds by sowing dates to ensure continuous colour.

Forward Planning for More Colour

Continue to plant bare-root trees, shrubs and roses while dormant, taking full advantage of these plants, which are considerably cheaper than containerised specimens and will establish better if planted now. Choose varieties with colourful stems, bark or winter flowers for year-round interest, the gaps in your borders will be obvious to you now and they will instantly add interest to your garden. While you're at it, introduce new hellebores, cyclamen or winter aconites to shady spots to expand your late winter colour displays.

Clean and Check Bird Boxes

Complete this task before nesting begins – the tenants will not only entertain you with their antics but provide invaluable pest control later in spring when collecting insects to feed to their chicks. For now, continue feeding birds regularly to maintain their populations through this transitional period.

MY ESSENTIAL DOS AND DON'TS

- + Divide snowdrops 'in the green' for naturalised drifts.
- + Create winter stem displays, either in the garden or in your house, from cut stems of coloured dogwood and willow.
- + Take evergreen cuttings while plants are dormant.
- + Surround emerging bulbs with fresh mulch.
- + Plant bare-root trees and shrubs for winter interest.
- + Photograph subtle late winter colours.
- + Clean bird boxes before the nesting season begins.
- + Remove tired perennial foliage to reveal early blooms.
- + Turn compost heaps if dry weather conditions allow.

- − Prune spring-flowering shrubs – they bloom on last year's wood and you risk removing the blooms.
- − Walk on soil that is frozen or waterlogged.
- − Rush outdoor seed sowing before soil warms and light levels increase.
- − Remove winter protection from tender plants too early – harsh frosts persist into spring.

Late Winter Mulching
Protecting and Feeding Early Performers

Late winter mulching isn't about the big borders yet – it's about emphasising the subtle stars already emerging. After carefully clearing only what truly detracts or may damage early blooms (dead leaves covering their crown, for example), mulch around snowdrops, hellebores and winter bulbs to create clean backgrounds while feeding the soil. This gentle intervention respects wildlife and soil health and celebrates early colour.

1 Consider the lie of the land
Remove thick layers of battered, brown leaves or collapsed stems that are impeding new growth. This isn't the time for a large scale cut back though, leave perennial structure where it stands to shelter overwintering insects and provide morning landing platforms for frost.

2 Choose your mulch
I reach for fine composted bark – its texture complements delicate winter flowers beautifully without overwhelming them. Alternatively, well-rotted garden compost from your own bins works brilliantly, provided it's fully decomposed (no recognisable bits) and fine-textured. Leafmould offers another excellent option. Avoid chunky materials that can overwhelm subtle late winter displays.

3 Minimal tidying, maximum impact
Resist the urge to tidy everything. Focus only on what actively spoils your enjoyment – perhaps a collapsed clump of rudbeckia foliage smothering emerging snowdrops, or soggy autumn leaves plastering down hellebore flowers. I do this by simply moving the debris deeper into the border, since wildlife depends on this 'untidy' habitat for hibernation. Major cutbacks wait until spring warms properly.

4 Mulch with precision
Apply mulch sparingly for now – just 1–2cm (½–¾in) around emerging bulbs and hellebore crowns. Create neat halos that frame flowers against clean, dark backgrounds. For areas expecting later bulbs such as daffodils or alliums, maintain similar restraint. The goal is subtle enhancement, allowing early flowers to shine, while protecting their roots from freeze-thaw cycles. You can top up the levels later.

5 Feed thoughtfully
As you mulch, consider adding bone meal around established hellebores or a light sprinkling of slow-release fertiliser near emerging daffodil foliage, but resist heavy feeding – overfed bulbs produce foliage at the expense of flowers. Late winter feeding should support existing growth, not stimulate premature new leaves.

6 Leave the borders uncovered
Resist the temptation to cut back and mulch entire borders now. Those seemingly untidy perennial remains protect countless overwintering creatures, from hedgehogs to beneficial insects. Additionally, many hollow stems provide nesting sites for solitary bees.

Prepping Your Seed-starting Arsenal
Getting equipment ready for spring

Patience now (I know it's hard to resist sowing right away!) can make the difference between seedling success and disappointment. Take this time to prepare equipment – after months of storage, trays may need cleaning, propagators require checking and compost stocks should be assessed, setting you up for smooth sowing sessions when spring arrives.

1 Make an inventory
Gather everything from last year – seed trays, modules, propagator lids, watering cans and tools. Check for damage: cracked trays can't hold water properly, while broken propagator lids won't maintain humidity. Make a list of replacements needed to prevent frustrating shopping trips when you should be sowing.

2 Clean thoroughly
Disease spores lurk on used equipment; slugs, too, if you've kept pots and trays outside. Wash everything in hot, soapy water, paying special attention to drainage holes that can harbour unwanted fungi. For stubborn deposits, soak in diluted bleach solution (1 part bleach to 10 parts water) for 10 minutes, then rinse thoroughly. Clean equipment dramatically improves seedling health.

3 Organise your workspace
Whether it's a windowsill, kitchen table or dedicated greenhouse bench, prepare your sowing station. Set up grow lights if using them, position propagators near light sources and ensure that there's a tap nearby so that you can water your plants easily. I organise labels (ordering more if I need them), scissors and other small tools into old jam jars so they're always within easy reach.

4 Check your compost supplies
Check your supplies, including partially used bags of compost that have been stored outside and may be compacted or waterlogged, which can prevent proper root development. Break up compacted material, sifting through the entire depth with your hands to aerate it. If it's very wet, leave your bags open on sunny days, or add grit when sowing to improve the structure.

5 Prepare labels in advance
Nothing's more frustrating than reaching for labels when your hands are covered in compost. Especially if last year's marker pen needs cleaning off them, too. Pre-cut lengths of twine, prepare plant markers, and make sure your permanent markers haven't dried out.

6 Get tooled up
Sharpen scissors to open seed packets cleanly, make sure the roses on your watering can or misters aren't clogged up, and check your heated propagator is still working. Ensure seed modules or cell trays fit properly into your propagator set-up, and that they're clean as a whistle. I always find that being prepared makes sure there are no interruptions once my seed-sowing enthusiasm kicks in properly, rather than wrestling with faulty, dirty or broken equipment.

Plant Directory

Page numbers in italics refer to illustrations.

A

Achillea 180
Aconitum carmichaelii (Arendsii Group) 'Arendsii' 110
Actaea simplex (Atropurpurea Group) 'Brunette' (Cimicifuga) 110
Afroaster 144
Agapanthus 163
Agastache 'Blackadder' 82, 83, 85, 118, 121
Alchemilla mollis 46, 58, 59, 88, 89, 98–100
Allium (ornamental onion) 77, 165, 244
　'Forelock' 94, 95
　hollandicum 'Purple Sensation' 46
　schubertii 78
　sphaerocephalon 86, 87
　'Summer Drummer' 76, 82, 83, 84, 161
　'Toabago' ('Spider') 78, 79, 80, 95
　'Yellow Fantasy' 58, 59
Amaryllis 165
Amelanchier × lamarckii 19, 25, 26, 27, 47, 77, 142, 143, 144
Ammi majus 163
Anemone 144, 163
　coronaria (De Caen group) 'Mister Fokker' 24, 25, 26, 48, 54, 55–7
　hupehensis var. japonica (Japanese anemone) 180, 181
　'Pamina' 95, 146, 158, 159
　× hybrid 'Honorine Jobert' 174
Anethum graveolens (dill) 'Mariska' 112, 113, 114, 184, 185
Angelica gigas 110, 111
Anthriscus sylvestris 'Ravenswing' 46
Aquilegia 135
Astrantia
　'Burgundy Manor' 95
　major subsp. involucrata 'Shaggy' 88, 89
Azalea, see Rhododendron

B

Baptisia 'Dutch Chocolate' 174
Betonica officinalis (betony) 'Hummelo' 76, 124, 125, 127, 212, 213
Betula 'Fascination' (silver birch) 200, 201
Bouteloua gracilis (mosquito grass) 86, 87
box 46

Briza
　media (quaking grass) 163
　minor 58, 59
Brunnera 100
　macrophylla 'Jack Frost' 59
Buddleia davidii (butterfly bush) 37, 133

C

Calamagrostis brachytricha (Korean feather reed grass) 108, 116, 117, 144, 160, 161, 185, 212, 213
Calendula (pot marigold) 41, 163
Callicarpa PEARL GLAM 146, 201
Camassia 165
　leichtlinii subsp. suksdorfii Caerulea Group 45, 60, 61
Canna 189
Caryopteris 37
Cenolophium denudatum 49, 76
Centaurea cyanus (cornflower) 65, 163
Centranthus ruber 'Albus' 88, 89
Cephalaria gigantea (giant scabious) 82, 83, 84
Clematis 38, 64, 103
　alpina 47
　cirrhosa var. purpurascens 'Freckles' 229
　'Etoile Violette' 77
　macropetala 47
Cleome 139
Colchicum 98, 99
　autumnale (autumn crocus) 144, 165
Consolida ajacis (larkspur) 163
Cornus (dogwood) 37, 146, 202, 241
　alba 'Sibirica' 241
　controversa 182, 183
　kousa 50
　sanguinea 'Midwinter Fire' 200
　sericea 'Flaviramea' 241
Coronilla valentina subsp. glauca 'Citrina' 201
Corylus avellana 'Contorta' (corkscrew hazel) 229
Cosmos 41, 97, 99, 135, 139
　bipinnatus 134
　'Apricotta' 148, 149
　'Rubenza' 144
Crocosmia (montbretia) 75, 97, 163
　'Lucifer' 92, 122, 123
　× crocosmiiflora 'George Davison' 118, 119, 121, 212, 213

Crocus 15, 36, 98, 165, 166
　olivieri subsp. balansae 'Orange Monarch' 16, 230, 231, 233, 236, 237, 238, 239
　sativus 98
　speciosus 98
　tommasinianus 16
　'Ruby Giant' 236, 237
Cyclamen 242
　coum 207, 226
　hederifolium 98, 144

D

Dahlia 8–10, 35, 97, 99, 108, 111, 142, 143, 152, 153, 155, 158, 159, 163, 174, 177, 192, 193, 217, 231
　Bishop varieties 97
　'Bishop of Canterbury' 152, 153, 154
　'Bright Eyes' 148, 149
　'Chat Noir' 186, 187
　'Labyrinth' 152, 153, 155, 186
　'Waltzing Mathilda' 109, 152, 153, 154, 155
daisy 77, 99, 117, 124, 129
Daphne bholua 'Jacqueline Postill' 227
Deschampsia cespitosa 49
　'Goldtau' 150, 151
Digitalis purpurea 88
Dipsacus laciniatus (teasel) 156, 157, 176, 186, 206, 207, 208, 209
Dryopteris erythrosora 16, 23

E

Echinacea (coneflower) 76, 97, 107, 135, 176, 241
　'Green Twister' 86, 87
　purpurea 'Magnus' 124, 125, 126, 128, 129
Echinops 110
Epimedium 20
　× perralchicum 'Fröhnleiten' 52, 53, 58, 59
　× versicolor 'Sulphureum' 20, 21, 210, 211
Eranthis hyemalis (winter aconite) 14–16, 207, 233, 242
　Cilicica Group (winter buttercups) 236, 237
Eryngium 97, 176
Erysimum cheiri (wallflower) 19, 176, 202, 230, 231

Erythronium
   dens-canis (dog's tooth violet) 20
   'Pagoda' 20, *21*
Euphorbia 9
   amygdaloides var. *robbiae* 46
Eurybia 144
Eutrochium purpureum 156, 157, *160*, 161, *184*, 185, 186, *187*

F
fern 226, 227, 235
   see also, Matteuccia, Polystichum, tree fern
Foeniculum vulgare (bronze fennel) 49, 91, 124, *128*, 129, *180*, *181*
   'Atropurpureum' 124, *125*, *127*
   'Purpureum' 77, 98, 99
forget-me-not 98
Fritillaria (fritillary) 165
   imperialis 45
   meleagris 48
fuschia dahlia 9

G
Galanthus (snowdrop) 15, 165, 201, 202, 204, 235, 241, 242, *243*, 244
   elwesii 'Maidwell' 204, *205*
   'Magnet' *234*, 235
   nivalis 16
   plicatus 'Three Ships' 204, *205*
   woronowii 204, *205*
Garrya elliptica 225
Geranium 110, 134, 135, 164
   endressii 100
   PATRICIA 74
   phaeum 100
   ROZANNE 100
   sylvaticum 100
Geum 164
   SCARLET TEMPEST 76
   'Totally Tangerine' 76, *115*
Gladiolus 176
   'Velvet Eyes' 212, *213*
grass, ornamental 35, 107, 108, 113, *116*, *117*, 134, 143, 144, *145*, 156, 157, *160*, 161, 163, 164, 174, *176*, 206, 207, *208*, *209*, 212, *213*, *234*, 235, 241
Grevillea rosmarinifolia 201

H
Hamamelis mollis (Chinese witch hazel) *182*, *183*, 202, 226, 241
Helenium 'Moerheim Beauty' 75, 76, *86*, 87

Helianthus annuus (sunflower) 41, *111*
   'Red Sun' *156*, 157
   'Ring of Fire' *160*, 161
   'Velvet Queen' *86*, 87
Helleborus (hellebore) 19, 31, 200, 201, 225, 226, 229, *234*, 235, 242, 244
   argutifolius 210, 211
   Gold Collection (MARLON) 235
   Ice 'n' Roses (MERLOT) 235
   niger Harvington hybrid 235
   orientalis 16, *17*
   ViV series (VICTORIA) 235
   × *hybridus* 'Yellow Lady' 235
   × *lemperii* HGC 'Liara' 235
Hemerocallis (day lily) 164
   'Stafford' 92, *93*
Heuchera 59
honeysuckle 64, 73, 103
Hordeum jubatum (foxtail barley) 163
Hydrangea 133
   arborescens 'Annabelle' 133

I
Ipomoea
   lobata (Spanish Flag) *128*, 129, *131*
   tricolor (morning glory) 103
Iris 225
   dwarf 166
   reticulata 226
   'Angela' *14*, 15
   'Benton' 46
   'Blue Note' *230*, 231
   'Pauline' *14*, 15, *230*, 231, *232*, *233*

J
jasmine 64, 103

K
Kalimeris 144

L
Lathyrus odoratus (sweet pea) 10, *90*, 91, 97, 99, 107, 218, 241
   'Black Knight' *90*, 91
   'Cupani' *90*, 91
   Grandiflora group 91
   'Henry Eckford' *90*, 91
   'Lord Nelson' *90*, 91
   'Matucana' *90*, 91
   Spencer group 91
Ligusticopsis wallichiana 185
lilac 45
lily of the valley 45
Lunaria annua 'Chedglow' 47

M
Magnolia 190, 229
Matthiola longipetala subsp. *bicornis* (night-scented stock) 99
Matteuccia (fern) 45, 47
   struthiopteris (ostrich fern) 22, 23, 46, 92, *93*, 122, 123
Miscanthus 174
   sinensis 122, 123
   'Malepartus' 144, *145*, *156*, 157, *178*, 179, 186, *187*, 206, 207, *208*, *209*
Monarda
   'Scorpion' 108
Muscari latifolium (grape hyacinth) 25, 26, *27*, *236*, 237

N
Narcissus (daffodil) 15, *18*, 19, 45, 53, 63, 165, 166, 231, 236, 244
   'Actaea' 18
   'Avalon' 24, *25*, *27*
   'Bella Estrella' 20, *21*
   bulbocodium 'Arctic Bells' 19, *238*, 239
   'Flower Drift' 24, *25*, 26
   'Lobularis' 18
   'Moonlight Sensation' 24, 25
   'Paperwhites' 165, *194*, 195
   'Regeneration' 25, 50, *51*
   'Tête-à-tête' *18*, 24, 25, 26, *27*, *238*, 239
   'Thalia' 46, 50, *51*
   'W. P. Milner' 18
nasturtium 41, 99
Nepeta × *faasenii* 134
nerine 98, 99, 165
Nicotiana 107, 134, 139
Nigella (love-in-a-mist) 135, 163

O
Ocimum basilicum 'Dark Opal' *178*, 179
Oenothera
   biennis (evening primrose) 98
   lindheimeri (gaura) 'Whirling Butterflies' 110, 135
Olea europaea (olive tree) 176, 186
Osmanthus × *burkwoodii* 201

P
Panicum
   'Sprinkles' *148*, 149
   virgatum 'Shenandoah' 108
pansy 166, 176, 202
Papaver (poppy) 65, 98, 99

rupifragum 'Flore Pleno' 78, *79*, *80*, *112*, 113
somniferum 'Lauren's Grape' 78, *79*, *80*, 99, 163
pea 'Alderman' *128*, *129*, *130*
pelargonium 37, 69, 189
Pennisetum 174
    orientale 'Flamingo' 83, *112*, *113*, *115*, 144, *145*, *156*, *157*, *184*, 185
Penstemon cultivars 133
peony 18, 99, 226
Philadelphus (mock orange) 99, 133
Phlomis russeliana (Turkish sage) 174, *206*, *207*, *209*, *212*, *213*
Physalis alkekengi (Chinese lantern) 110
Pieris 226
Polystichum (fern)
    setiferum (Divisilobum Group) 'Herrenhausen' 46, *52*, *53*, *182*, *183*, *204*, *205*, *210*, *211*, *234*, *235*
Primula vulgaris (primrose) *30*, 31
Prunus 191
    × *subhirtella* 'Autumnalis Rosea' 229

R

Ratibida columnifera f. *pulcherrima* (Mexican hat) 113, *115*, 179
Rhododendron 32, 50, 190
    luteum 46, *182*, 183
Rodgersia
    pinnata 'Chocolate Wing' 23
    podophylla 'Braunlaub' *22*, 23, 60, *61*, *92*, *93*
Rosa 37, 38, 74, 77, 97, 99, 163, 164, 242
    'Etoile Violette' 103
    'Madame Alfred Carrière' 103
    NIGHT OWL *92*, *93*
    shrub rose *22*, 23, 97
    THE SIMPLE LIFE 74, 201
    × *odorata* 'Mutabilis' 74
Rubus thibetanus 200
Rudbeckia 35, 99, 244
    fulgida var. *sullivantii* 'Goldsturm' 108
    subtomentosa 'Henry Eilers' 144, *145*, 150, *151*

S

Salix (willow) 241
    alba var. *vitellina* 'Britzensis' (coral bark dogwood) 226, 241
Salvia 9, 35, 41, 76, 77, 97, 133, 164
    'Amethyst' 76
    'Amistad' 108, 144, 173
    atriplicifolia (Russian sage) 133
    'Blue Spire' (*Perovskia*) 110
    'Caradonna' 76
    'Mainacht' 100
    uliginosa 174, 186, *187*
Sanguisorba 99
    officinalis 160, 161
Sarcococca confusa (sweet box) 19, 199, 241
Scilla
    sardensis *30*, 31
    siberica 'Alba' *30*, 31
Sedum 241
    takesimense ATLANTIS *210*, 211
Selinum wallichiana 185
Sesleria autumnalis (Autumn moor grass) *94*, 95
Sorbus aria 'Lutescens' 144, 179, *180*, *181*, 200
Stachys byzantina 'Purple Rain' 49
Stipa gigantea 74
Symphyotrichum (aster) 134, 144, *163*
    'Vasterival' *116*, 117, *206*, 207

T

Tagetes (marigold) 139
    'Burning Ember' 65, *128*, *129*, 130
Taxus (yew) 202
Tellima grandiflora 46
Teucrium hircanicum 'Paradise Delight' 158, *159*
Thalictrum 'Elin' *152*, *153*, *156*, 157
Tithonia 35
tomato 35, 143
Trachelospermum 107
    jasminoides *158*, *159*, 186, *187*, 227
tree fern 189
Trifolium (clover)
    rubens 78, *79*, *80*, 113, *115*, 148, *149*, *178*, 179
Tulipa 44, 45, 47, *47*, 50, *51*, 54, 55, 63, 165, 166, 189, 191
    'Apricot Foxx' 47, 54, *55–7*
    'Avignon' 32
    'Ayaan' 54, *55–7*
    'Ballerina' 28, *29*, 32
    'Banja Luka' 28, *29*, 48
    'Bourbon Street' 28, *29*
    'Cairo' 32, *33*, 54, *55–7*
    clusiana 48
    'Continental' 28, *29*, 54, *55–7*
    Darwin hybrids 28, 48, 54
    'Devenish' 32, *33*
    Fosteriana group 28, 48
    Greigii group 28
    'Havran' 47
    Kaufmanniana group 28
    'Louvre Orange' 32, *33*
    'Oakheart' 32, *33*
    'Orange Marmalade' 50, *51*
    'Purple Heart' 32, *33*
    'Queen of Night' 32
    'Ridgedale' 32
    'Slawa' 32, 54, *55–7*
    'Sonnet' 28, *29*, 47
    sylvestris 48
    'Synaeda Orange' 54, *55–7*
    tarda 48
    'Uncle Tom' 32
    Viridiflora Group 49, 50
    'Green Mile' 20, *21*, 50, *51*

V

Verbascum 77, 99
    chaixii 'Sixteen Candles' 118, *119*, 121
Verbena (vervain)
    bonariensis 76, 83, 98, 118, *119*, *128*, 129
    hastata f. *rosea* 118, *119*
    officinalis 'Bampton' 121
    × *baileyana* 'Purple Haze' 77, *120*, 121, 150, *151*
Veronicastrum 75, 99
    virginicum 'Fascination' 83, *122*, *123*
Viburnum
    opulus (guelder rose) 'Xanthocarpum' 146
    tinus 241
    × *bodnantense* 'Dawn' 227
Viola 19, 176, 202, 230, 231
    'Sorbet Honeybee' *230*, 231
    'Sorbet XP Morpho' *230*, 231
    'Tiger Eye Red' *230*, 231

W

wisteria 98, 99

Z

Zinnia 65, 99
    elegans 134
    'Queen Lime Red' *148*, 149

General Index

A
acid soil 183
animals and pests, protection from 32, 37
annuals 28, 35, 50, 65, 87, 99, 103, 129, 134, 135, 139, 147, 149, 163, 179, 185, 241
architectural interest 16, 20, 23, 31, 35, 45, 49, 59, 60, 76, 83, 87, 92, 95, 97, 108, 110, 111, 113, 117, 123, 124, 143, 147, 149, 157, 165, 174, 176, 177, 179, 183, 185, 186, 191, 199, 200, 201, 204, 207, 211, 212, 235, 239, 241, 244
aspect and conditions 8, 9, 16, 19, 23, 31, 32, 49, 53, 60, 78, 83, 88, 91, 97, 108, 110, 117, 118, 123, 124, 129, 149, 153, 157, 158, 161, 179, 180, 183, 185, 207, 211, 235, 236, 239

B
bees, see wildlife
berries 26, 146, 183, 199–201
biennials 157, 163, 207
birds, see wildlife
bog gardens 60, 191
borders 35, 65, 66, 74, 83, 88, 91, 95, 97, 107, 111, 113, 117, 118, 123, 129, 133, 143, 153, 158, 174, 179, 189, 211, 236, 244
'borrowed brightness' 201
bulbs 15, 16, 20, 25, 26, 28, 31, 32, 36, 37, 47, 50, 53, 54, 59, 60, 65, 78, 83, 87, 95, 98, 99, 143, 144, 147, 165, 166, 176, 177, 192, 195, 200, 202, 204, 225, 226, 229, 231, 233, 236, 239, 242, 244
  autumn-flowering 98, 99
butterflies, see wildlife

C
climate-consciousness 191
climbers 38, 47, 63–5, 73, 77, 91, 92, 97, 99, 103, 129, 133, 158, 164, 186, 201, 215, 217, 218, 227, 229
coastal gardens 18, 174, 201
cold frames 91, 163, 218
companion planting 32, 50, 57, 129, 134, 149, 153, 161, 231
compost 35–8, 41, 50, 54, 59, 64, 66, 69, 97, 98, 100, 133, 135, 136, 139, 153, 158, 163, 164, 166, 169, 183, 186, 190, 192, 195, 211, 217, 218, 231, 236, 239, 242, 244, 247

conditions, see aspect and conditions
containers, see pots
corms 25
cottage gardens 78, 88, 124, 127, 149
crown-lifting 183
Cupani, Francisco 91
cuttings 103, 133, 135, 165, 179, 241, 242

D
daffodils, indoor winter display 195
deadheading 8, 50, 59, 63, 65, 78, 87, 88, 92, 95, 97, 99, 113, 118, 124, 129, 139, 147, 149, 150, 153, 158, 161, 163, 166, 179, 180, 231, 239
deciduous trees and shrubs 18, 20, 53, 88, 92, 113, 163, 183, 191, 201, 217
disease 37, 38, 54, 64, 65 69, 92, 100, 164, 165, 191, 212, 217, 247
dividing
  bulbs 50, 204, 241, 242
  perennials 8, 36, 59, 60, 63–5, 78, 88, 92, 118, 123, 147, 150, 157, 161, 163, 164, 186
drainage, see soil
drought 20, 23, 53, 60, 83, 87, 88, 100, 110, 113, 133, 136, 207, 211, 235

E
Eckford, Henry 91
ecological value 76, 150, 180, 191, 227
edible plants 65, 92, 103, 113, 124, 129, 153, 179, 185
evergreens 16, 19, 32, 53, 78, 95, 150, 158, 174, 176, 183, 186, 200–04, 211, 212, 215, 217, 235, 241, 242

F
feed and fertiliser 26, 28, 38, 50, 54, 65, 69, 91, 97, 99, 100, 139, 163, 169, 186, 239, 244
figure-of-eight knot 64, 103
flower gap analysis 189
fragrance 18, 19, 20, 25, 28, 45, 49, 50, 69, 73, 78, 83, 88, 91, 92, 99, 107, 110, 129, 139, 143, 150, 158, 179, 183, 195, 199, 202, 218, 225, 227, 231
freeze-thaw cycle 35, 65, 97, 111, 117, 135, 153, 161, 165, 169, 173, 179, 186, 189, 192, 199, 215, 217, 218, 242, 244

frost interest 111, 113, 176, 185, 200, 202, 203, 207–11, 231, 233
  see also, freeze-thaw cycle

G
gaps in borders 66
grass, see lawn maintenance
greenhouses 35, 41, 163, 165, 189, 215, 217

H
Hampton Court
  pruning hack 100
  show garden 235
hardening off 37, 41, 65
herbaceous 16, 35, 73, 200
  see also, perennials
heritage varieties 91, 129
hibernation 190, 191, 241, 244
humus 20, 59, 60, 88, 92, 95, 183, 235
hybrids 20, 28, 48, 50, 54, 78, 121, 135, 150, 174, 226, 235

I
insects, see wildlife

J
Jelitto Seeds 124

L
lasagne, of bulbs 166, 167
  see also, layering of bulbs
lawn maintenance 36, 65, 73, 107, 134, 165, 190, 191, 217
layering
  in borders 53, 74, 76, 77, 83, 109, 124, 144, 147, 153, 158, 174, 183, 201, 211
  of bulbs 18, 20, 25, 26, 28, 47, 54, 57, 165–7, 202, 231, 236
  to propagate climbers 103
leaf mould 20, 59, 183, 211, 235, 244

M
maintenance, of garden structures 215, 217
  see also, lawn, support structures, tools
manure 35, 38, 164, 218
meadow 18, 48, 113, 185
Mediterranean climate 87
microclimate 9, 201
moving plants 169

General Index 253

mulch 23, 35, 36, 38, 50, 53, 60, 64–6, 95, 100, 123, 133, 135, 136, 153, 158, 166, 180, 183, 186, 189, 191, 192, 204, 211, 212, 215, 217, 226, 235, 239, 242, 244

N
nematodes 37
Nilsson, Magnus B. 124
nitrogen 129, 135

O
organic matter, *see* compost, humus, leaf mould, manure, mulch
Oudolf, Piet 124
overcrowding, *see* dividing
overwintering 35–7, 179, 190, 207, 217, 218, 244

P
perennials 8, 16, 28, 35, 36, 46, 48, 49, 50, 53, 60, 63, 65, 73–89, 92, 95, 97–100, 107, 108, 124, 128, 133–5, 144, 147, 157, 161, 163, 165, 174, 176, 179, 180, 191, 207, 226, 242
perfume, *see* fragrance
pest control 7, 37, 65, 92, 129, 163, 164, 166, 186, 242, 247
    see also, disease
planting 7, 16, 19, 26, 28, 31, 50, 54, 59, 63, 66, 73, 91, 107, 113, 118, 149, 150, 157, 163, 169, 177, 189, 191, 201, 207, 217, 218, 239
    see also, layering, propagators, seeds
pollinators 60, 65, 78, 83, 87, 88, 95, 113, 118, 123, 124, 129, 149, 150, 153, 161, 165, 179, 180, 186, 200, 227, 231, 236
ponds 165
potassium 38, 54, 91, 99, 139, 153, 163
pots 8, 9, 15, 16, 18–20, 25, 26, 32, 36, 37, 41, 45, 47–9, 54, 64–6, 69, 97, 99, 113, 133, 135, 136, 139, 147, 149, 153, 155, 163, 165, 166, 174, 176, 177, 179, 186, 189, 192, 195, 200, 202, 211, 215, 217, 218, 231, 236, 239, 242, 247
prairie-style planting 87, 118, 124, 127
propagation, *see* cuttings, layering
propagators 35, 41, 163, 247
protection, *see* animals and pests, freeze-thaw cycle, support structures
pruning 35, 37, 38, 63, 65, 98, 99, 100, 113, 135, 139, 158, 165, 180, 186, 191, 241

R
regeneration, of borders 124
Royal Horticultural Society (RHS)
    Award of Garden Merit 20, 91
    Chelsea Plant of the Year, 2019 211
    Hampton Court Palace Garden Festival 100, 235
rooting hormone 133

S
scent, *see* fragrance
seedlings, development stages 41, 65, 113, 124, 129, 163
seeds 31, 91, 135, 165, 179, 185, 189, 212, 218, 242, 247
    seed heads 35, 76, 78, 83, 87, 95, 97, 107, 110, 111, 113, 117, 123, 124, 135, 143, 147, 149, 150, 157, 161, 165, 174, 176, 177, 180, 185, 191, 199, 200, 202, 207, 211, 212
    self-seeding 31, 47, 48, 83, 88, 95, 98–100, 107, 113, 118, 124, 129, 157, 179, 180, 185, 207, 236
    sowing 41, 49, 63, 65, 87, 91, 99, 113, 135, 163, 241, 242, 247
shade 20, 23, 32, 59, 60, 77, 88, 110, 123, 124, 135, 136, 157, 180, 183, 185, 204, 212, 235, 236, 239
    see also, aspect and conditions
shelter 59, 60, 92, 129, 147, 163, 174, 177, 189, 191, 201, 207, 215, 217, 231, 235, 244
shrubs 23, 32, 37, 63, 65, 73, 97–9, 133, 135, 136, 144, 146, 147, 165, 183, 186, 191, 200, 201, 215, 217, 235, 241, 242
slugs and snails, *see* pest control
soil 25, 48, 97, 113, 161, 183, 207, 235
    improvement 35, 60, 83, 87, 158, 164, 186, 189, 190, 217
    well-drained 20, 28, 50, 59, 78, 83, 88, 95, 117, 118, 129, 149, 158, 161, 163, 164, 179, 180, 183, 185, 186, 190, 204, 207, 211, 235
sowing, *see* seeds
staking, *see* support structures
stems, colour interest in winter 241, 242
storm damage, *see* shelter, support structures
structures, *see* architectural interest, soil, support structures
sun, *see* aspect and conditions
support structures 36, 63, 65, 87, 97, 99, 103, 124, 129, 134, 135, 158, 161, 164, 180, 186, 189, 195, 217
swales 191

T
textures 20, 23, 25, 28, 32, 45, 46, 49, 53, 54, 59, 60, 65, 66, 76, 78, 83, 87, 88, 95, 97, 110, 117, 121, 124, 144, 146, 147, 149, 150, 153, 157, 158, 161, 173, 174, 177, 179, 180, 185, 186, 204, 211, 212, 229, 235, 239, 244
tools 36, 38, 63, 100, 103, 134, 164, 169, 189, 217, 218, 221, 247
training, *see* climbers
transplanting 169
    see also, dividing
trees 8, 16, 18, 20, 26, 31, 37, 45, 53, 73, 77, 88, 107, 133, 144, 163, 176, 180, 183, 186, 189, 191, 200, 201, 215, 217, 229, 235, 242
tubers 236
    dahlia 35, 97, 99, 153, 158, 186, 192, 217, 231
tulip fire disease 54, 165, 191

V
vegetables 65, 103, 129
Viridiflora Group 20

W
watering 26, 41, 54, 64–6, 69, 78, 88, 100, 110, 129, 133, 135, 136, 139, 147, 149, 158, 163, 169, 183, 189, 195, 207, 218, 225, 231, 235, 236
weeding 7, 8, 60, 65, 66
wildlife 8, 9, 19, 35, 37, 45, 65, 73, 78, 83, 84, 87, 97, 107, 113, 118, 121, 124, 129, 135, 146, 150, 157, 161, 165, 174, 176, 177, 190, 191, 199–202, 207, 212, 217, 241, 242, 244
    see also, animals, protection from; overwintering; pollinators
wind damage, *see* shelter, support structures
woodland 20, 31, 32, 50, 59, 60, 110, 183, 195, 201, 204, 211, 235
worm action 35, 163, 164

The Author

Ann-Marie Powell is a multi-award-winning garden designer, television presenter, journalist and author, who divides her time between designing innovative gardens for private clients, companies and charities, and enthusing people about gardening through her books, television appearances, talks and articles in national newspapers and magazines. In 2024, Ann-Marie was awarded Children's Choice and BBC People's Choice awards for her Octavia Hill inspired garden at RHS Chelsea Flower Show. She shares her own passion for gardening via her loyal Instagram community @myrealgarden.

The Photographer

Julie Skelton specialises in garden photography, taking pictures for the image libraries of a number of notable UK gardens, designers and RHS garden shows. She is a member of the Garden Media Guild and has had photographs published internationally in books and magazines.

Acknowledgements

Writing a book about gardening feels rather like tending a garden itself – it takes a village, and I've been blessed with a particularly good one.

My heartfelt thanks go first to Janet and Peter Morgan, who encouraged me to attend horticultural college all those years ago and cheered me on throughout my studies. Your belief in me laid the foundation for everything that followed.

To my husband Jules, who has been my steadfast companion through decades of garden adventures and has supported me wholeheartedly throughout the writing of this book. Your understanding and encouragement have meant the world.

I'm deeply grateful to Julie Skelton, whose talent and enthusiasm have been extraordinary. She has captured the garden exactly as I see it, creating sumptuous photographs that bring these pages to life. Her energy and constant support over many months have been both a tremendous help and a genuine joy.

Special thanks to those who helped shape this book along the way: Alice Graham and Laura Bulbeck, whose insights were invaluable and Zia Allaway for her sensitive and skilful copy-editing. Sarah Pyke for the beautiful book design, Isabel Eeles for art direction, Lesley Malkin for the proofread, Amanda Leigh for the index and Rohana Yusof in production.

To my wonderful team at Ann-Marie Powell Gardens – particularly Mary Guinness and Penny Walker – thank you for your constant encouragement and for believing in this project even when my own confidence wavered.

I'm grateful too to the many nurseries, head gardeners and fellow horticulturalists whose knowledge and inspiration have enriched my understanding of plants and gardens over the years.

Finally, to the remarkable international community of My Real Gardeners who have shared this journey with me through all its seasons. Your support, wisdom, and friendship have shaped not only my garden but made this book possible. I will never forget.

Without you all, my colourful garden life and career wouldn't be what it is today. I'm tremendously grateful.